Palestinian Women

Rising above Limitations, Expectations, & Conditions

Sadiqua Hamdan

Contents

Foreword

For the last few decades, Palestinian women have been the focus of several studies. For many activists, sociologists, and politicians, Palestinian women's determination and resilience in their unabated and ongoing struggle for freedom, justice, and peace under the gravest hardships constituted a phenomenon worth studying, emulating, or admiring, depending on the party conducting the research.

Among the most enthusiastic researchers in the field are young Palestinian women, such as Sadiqua Hamdan, who were raised outside of Palestine. As these young women start to dig for their roots, they are amazed at the success of Palestinian women in defying the seemingly insurmountable obstacles they face every day. Their struggle to liberate themselves and their country, to protect their families, and to guarantee a dignified life and future for their people as a whole has become a source of inspiration for these young researchers. Due to their family and social links, these women are able to study Palestinian women in the correct context, thus arriving at an in-depth understanding of them and the driving force behind their inner strength and resilience, which enables them to rise above their limitations and the harsh reality of their lives.

We cannot fully understand the situation of Palestinian women without comprehending the dimensions of the historical catastrophes that have befallen Palestine since the beginning of the last century and especially since 1948. The Israeli occupation is one landmark within a series of events that looms threateningly over every single aspect of Palestinian life. Women, the bearers and guardians of human life, are always at the forefront in enduring the consequences of national disasters. Palestinian women have played an outstanding role in confronting decades of aggression, dispossession, impoverishment, and denial of rights and identity. Women from all walks of life have faced these challenges with courage and resilience and never have shied away from mobilizing their efforts and resources and sacrificing their well-being to address them. Mothers of prisoners and martyrs are one example of the courage of Palestinian women under adversity. Holding their heads high and suppressing their suffering with a heavy heart, they endure with patience and equanimity the saga of their sons' hunger strikes, even as they are life threatening.

Palestinian women realized early on that national liberation goes hand in hand with liberation from the fetters of ignorance, poverty, and traditions that discriminate against them. Naturally all these fetters are interlinked. The occupation, which plays a hegemonic role over every aspect of Palestinian life and natural resources, leads to poverty. It also threatens education through its closure of schools and universities and its restriction of access to them and through its intervening in school curricula. Under occupation, therefore, there is limited room for maneuvering in order to maintain a vibrant society that is able to withstand the grave hardships to which it is subjected. Yet Palestinian women and the Palestinian people as a whole have been able to do so by uniting their efforts, resources, creativity, determination, and resilience and by prioritizing the needs of the moment. A delicate balance between priorities has allowed women to make a marked impact on the course of events. While struggling for national liberation, they never have lost the vision of their struggle for social justice and equality.

Palestinian women have confronted all the problems that emanate from the occupation and the continual process of dispossession and denial of identity and rights by mobilizing themselves into groups, unions, voluntary societies, and grassroots committees that are active on all fronts and in every part of Palestine in an attempt at to address the major issues confronting Palestinian women.

The quest for education is another means by which women have been able to rise above their limitations. The number of female university students and graduates in Palestine is striking. Education invests women with self-confidence and promises them a better quality of life and financial independence. Many women currently are breaking ground in their professional fields and in their public positions, and are held in high esteem in their society. In the cultural field, women are also making outstanding contributions that are being recognized nationally and internationally.

As the Palestinian people are challenged in regard to their history, identity, and religious rights, many Palestinian women find solace in their religion and choose to affirm their identity by adhering to its tenets and practices and by holding on to positive values in their traditions. This often is reflected in their appearance and dress, which is, unfortunately, often misinterpreted as regression in their status; in reality, however, it is merely one means of expressing their identity and protecting it from the unabated onslaught against it and against their history, traditions, and beliefs.

Sadiqua Hamdan's interviews and personal testimonies undoubtedly will illuminate this book's readers and present them with fresh insight into the lives of Palestinian women and their ability to rise above their suffering to build a dignified and peaceful future for themselves and their people.

Rima Tarazi

Introduction

Village Women

"A jug can pour forth only what it contains."
—— Arab proverb

"Had we known the solution to saving the Roman Empire, we would be in a better position to save our looks. But if the empire could not stop from falling, how are we to stop our breasts from doing the same?" Um Omar asks the other women elders in the village one evening.[1] This is one of many lighthearted conversations that take place in Palestinian women's circles. However, not everyone is as vocal or straightforward as Um Omar, an eighty-eight-year-old mother of five who never has had any type of formal education.

"May God have mercy on my father, who did not teach me how to read," she says.

1

Um Omar was twenty-four years old when she married her one and only husband. But she was not the first wife. She was the second wife to a man who was eighteen years her senior. Um Omar blends in with the village's culture, although a change of clothes could make her appear to be a visitor. Her gray hair, once as golden as summer's wheat, is now fully covered with a *mandeela* (headscarf). The blue pigment in her eyes matches the sky stone of heaven, lapis lazuli. Her round white face highlights her bright-red cheeks. She is a wonderful mother to her children, who all but one inherited their father's dark skin and brown eyes.

Um Omar has fond memories of her marriage and talks about her husband's first wife as if she were naturally part of the landscape. "For our honeymoon he took me to Beirut for one whole month." This line she occasionally repeats throughout the conversation, as if it just happened a month ago. The first wife lives in one room of the house, and Um Omar has her own room. "He always met the call of duty with me. He never fell short of providing for me." It wasn't until years later, after enough money was earned, that she had her own house and he lived with her permanently.

Um Omar has an incredibly good-humored laugh that can be recognized anywhere, without seeing her in person. She immerses herself in every story she tells, playing the role of each character. It is as if she is standing behind the curtain of each scene, watching and simultaneously describing what is going on.

She adds her own commentary as she sees fit. There are many storytellers in the village but few who can command the room's attention as Um Omar does.

"Let me tell you something," she says to the women elders, interrupting her own story and recalling details of another. "Khalid was a mule for doing what he did. The worms of vinegar are of the vinegar itself.[2] His whole family should not be spoken to because of his actions."

A few ladies agree with her while two shake their heads in disapproval. "Only God can hold him accountable. Shake hands with him, but count your fingers afterwards. Is it necessary to cut off his family for his wrongdoing?" asks Um Hasan.

There is no specific home, date, or time designated to the weekly women's gathering, nor a special day or time. None of the five elderly ladies sitting in this room can read or write. None of them ever has driven a car. Most of the women know how use a mobile phone but do not know the meaning of the word *text,* nor do they want to learn how to check voice messages. The closest they can come to pronouncing these words is *teck-est* and *voice habal* (*"habal"* means "foolishness" in Arabic). The invention of the microwave, however, makes them very happy.

Um Omar, like the rest of the women in the room, is street smart. She has memorized the bus routes and schedules in the area. Her loyalty lies within the network she's established over the years, not to strangers in the *souk* (market), who speak of better deals. She doesn't act poor or rich but always has looked for ways to increase the family income. Um Omar has a designated *thoub,* or traditional Palestinian dress, that is solely used whenever she goes to the city *souk* to sell vegetables. "My whole wardrobe used to consist of three *thwaab.*[3] That's it," she says. "I had to wash and rewash them over and over again for years, by hand, until there was enough money to buy more dresses."

Evolution of a Palestinian Woman

Over the past seventy years, the lives of Palestinian women have changed in many ways, while other aspects of their lives have remained the same. Prior to the 1940s, very little information was documented about Palestinian women. Most available literature that mentions the word "Palestine" focuses on religion, displacement, or the Israeli-Palestinian conflict. The phrase "Palestinian woman" reveals information in the context of domestic violence, religious oppression, or displacement.

Hilma Granqvist, a Finnish anthropologist, was one of the few people who studied Palestinian women. In the 1920s she originally went to Palestine to conduct research in order to find the Jewish ancestors mentioned in Scripture.[4] Instead she found a distinct culture that she wanted to observe—the Palestinians. She changed her thesis and spent three years in a village near Bethlehem. [5]

During this period, a typical Palestinian woman's main purpose in life was to marry, give birth to many children, cook, clean, and work the fields. Her priority was to find a mate, but she had no say regarding whom she could marry. The task of choosing her husband was left to her father and male relatives.[6] A married Palestinian woman had no more independence than she'd had during her single years when she lived with her family. In other words her role of obeying her parents was transferred to obeying her husband. "The shadow of a man and not the shadow of a wall" is a well-known Arabic proverb that best describes this period of a Palestinian woman's life.[7]

A burgeoning literature on Palestinian lifestyles emerged in the 1970s, but it remained confined within the context of conflict. Many authors were concerned with the displacement of Palestinian refugees and the effects of war on Palestinian women. During this era articles began to explore domestic and national abuses toward Palestinian women.

Since the 1970s, one might hope that the lives of Palestinian women would been examined in greater detail. Sadly that is not the case. Even in the last five years, for example, few reports discuss Palestinian women, and the subject matters are limited to women's displacement from or within their homeland, their lack of freedom, religious oppression, and domestic violence. In addition many people in the Western world assume that Palestinian women are submissive and uneducated and live lifestyles that are similar to Arab women in surrounding countries.

Where is the literature that shines a light on Palestinian women's thoughts, opinions, and beliefs regarding their status in society, individualism, roles within the community, marriage, education, and the labor market? What little has been published regarding these topics is not recent, although we're beginning to see more information surrounding highly educated Palestinian women who are not actively working due to high unemployment rates.

My Background

I was born to Palestinian parents who immigrated to the United States in the early 1970s. I grew up in the United States but lived in my parents' homeland from age nine to twelve. This was the first time my four brothers and I had met our grandparents and extended family. My father had just finished building a home in Beitin, a Palestinian village located near Ramallah in the West Bank. After we moved there, my brothers and I began to learn Arabic and all things related to the culture. Three years later, however, my parents made the difficult decision to move back to the United States after the 1988 *Intifadah* (Palestinian uprising).[8]

My dad came to the United States when he was twenty-five years old and hoped he could build more for himself in America than he had in the village where he had grown up. He arrived in New York on September 9, 1971 with two packed suitcases and one hundred dollars. He had no car and no driver's license and spoke no English. Unlike his homeland, this place did not allow him to feel God everywhere. In his village he had heard the name of God on the tip of everyone's tongue. "*Insh'Allah*" was spoken by anyone who wanted God to will something to happen. Where my father comes from, dentists, doctors, policemen, grandparents, and shopkeepers all stop in unison to thank God five times a day. For ten minutes they pause whatever they are doing, pull out a prayer rug, and pray. "Stop. Drop. Pray." would make a great advertisement on behalf of God in my dad's homeland. While my dad never has considered himself a man of religious actions, he is accustomed to seeing others act in the name of God.

Where my dad comes from, everything has meaning and value, including a person's name. He was raised in Beitin, a Palestinian village where it was customary to name your firstborn son after your father. My dad was not the first son in his family, nor was he the last. He grew up with seven siblings—five sisters and two brothers. Living quarters were tight; the family home had two rooms, plus a kitchen, a patio, and an outhouse. Later the home would be expanded to include an in-house toilet and a room off the patio where guests would be more comfortable to enjoy mint tea or strong Turkish coffee.

Where my father comes from, if society deems you to be credible and respectful, you receive high praises, and the streets beneath your feet are magically lined with gold. If you have a bad reputation, however, the community secretly curses you behind your back. Not only are you labeled a donkey, but also your parents are considered bigger asses for not teaching you to be a respectable citizen.

The larger issue is that an outside authority tells folks like my dad, a man born in Beitin, that their homeland does not belong to them. Someone else told my dad how to live his life—where he could work, which roads he was permitted to use, and what time he had to be at home. This authority did not care that my dad opened his own coffee shop after he graduated from high school. It was a small *dukaan* that could accommodate up to fifteen people. His menu was simple. There were no falafel sandwiches or ice cream, but customers could have their pick of tea, coffee, or soda for three *qirsh*. His establishment quickly turned into a late-night gathering place for card-playing smokers. He also was the first person in Beitin to buy a color television. And since non-family members of the opposite sex are discouraged from mingling, my dad also was the first person to host a ladies' night every Wednesday evening. But again this authority did not care about his entrepreneurial spirit.

My mother, Lamia, known as "the beautiful one," has her own story, but she refuses to speak it out loud. I had to learn it from someone else. When I did, I had to figure out how to relate to a mother whose father was, for the most part, absent from her childhood because he could only find financial security outside of the country. It was the only way he could provide for the family. How could I understand my mother's psyche when she had to walk daily to the communal village well and back home, carrying jugs of water on her shoulders, because the well was the only source of drinking, cooking, and bathing water? What does responsibility feel like when a girl is ten years old, when at that age life commands her to milk cows every morning before going to school, as my mother had to do? How important was education in the grand scheme of things when her two sisters, brother, mother, and extended family waited for breakfast (a glass of milk, homemade bread, and a slice of tomato) before carrying on with work and daily chores? How could my mother make me understand that she had married into the Hamdan family and moved to the United States with the hope of passing on Palestine's culture to my four brothers and me?

The only way for me to understand was by going to the best source available—my mother's mother, Aziza. My grandmother turned eighty-five years old before she was ready to talk about my mother and her own life experiences. These stories unfolded during my visit to Beitin in September 2011.

The name "Aziza" is of Arabic origin and means "precious." I call her *Sitti*, the Arabic village word for "my grandmother." Although, as a child, Sitti stood true to her given name, someone always was telling her she wasn't precious. As she grew into womanhood, Sitti hid from her thoughts, her voice, and her own shadow. She didn't want to draw attention to herself, not even from the rays of sun that bless the entire land. But no one looks at an olive tree and asks it why it hides its fruit. It blossoms when it's ready and under the right conditions. As Sitti grew up, it did not occur to her that this could be the case for herself.

Sitti knew that modern-day wars were fought over simple things, like the length and fit of a shirt—the shorter the sleeve, the greater the misfortune. Many times she wanted to ask the one-hundred-year-old fig tree in the village center what it was like to be born from nothing and grow into something. She wanted to know what it was like to bear fruit every year and not expect anything in return. She wanted to know what it was like to be respected for what she could give—no more and no less.

Sitti grew up believing that it is better to live "in the shadow of a man and not the shadow of a wall." This proverb had circled around the village since the land was overrun with weeds and ruble. It encouraged a girl to get married rather than be alone. "It is better to be educated and stand on your own two feet," she told me in confidence. "If you are going to overcome shadows in your life, they might as well be your own and no one else's. You can live your own life with or without a husband."

At the age of eighteen, Sitti became a bride out of obligation, not love. Her brother Mustafa was interested in marrying a young woman, and this woman's parents agreed on one condition—that their son would marry Mustafa's sister, Aziza. In their eyes this was a better deal than the initial offer. And so it was written. Sitti's fate was sealed by her brother, uncle, and future father-in-law. Sadly I learned that my grandpa, Seedi, was not the generous, caring, and loving man I grew up knowing—at least not when it came to Sitti's welfare.

Seedi and Sitti's hearts were not set on each other, but they could not go against their parents' wishes. Seedi and Sitti married and lived in Seedi's parents' house. From that day forward, and for many years, Sitti's in-laws and husband told her what time to leave the house, what time she had to be back, what to wear, and what she was worth. As long as Sitti obeyed her new family, properly rolled grape leaves filled with rice and spices, and worked harder than an animal, her position in society was safe. Sitti wasn't asked if she would like to go out for fun, nor did her husband shower her with gifts. No one asked her about her opinions of the war or complimented her on her wonderful ability to take ordinary ingredients and turn them into delightful meals. Eventually Sitti gained respect in her household by standing up for herself. She allowed kindness and forgiveness to guide her through life, rather than retribution and bitterness. Sitti did not tolerate a poorly prepared meal nor did she allow bitterness to lead her heart.

There are stories from her early life that were hard for her to speak out loud; she also believes they are no longer of importance. Instead she wanted to share stories no one hears in the news, such as the day the villagers came into contact with a forbidden animal.

She told me that in March of the previous year, twenty wild pigs were covertly released into the fields during the middle of the night. When the villagers awoke the next morning, they found the leaves on their trees shaved off and their land trampled. No one in the area ever had come into contact with a wild pig—dead or alive. It wasn't easy for the villagers to figure out how to get rid of them. Sitti, however, would do anything necessary to protect the fruit trees and didn't wait for a community decision. Instead she went to the local market and bought enough rat poison to kill an elephant. She placed bowls of poisoned water outside, thinking the pigs would be thirsty after their midnight run of the land.

The next morning she found two dead pigs in the backyard. The pigs were incredibly heavy. Sitti attempted to lift one, but it wouldn't budge. She tried to push it, but it wouldn't move. Finally she thought, *Well, I'll just burn you here.* She didn't know, however, the length of time it would take to cremate a pig and believed it could be no different than burning trash or leaves. She hoped the pigs would quickly go up in flames, but instead she ended up with two barbecued pigs! She unintentionally had made a forbidden meal, and it had taken her all day to prepare it. Finally two young men came by to transport the carcasses to the local landfill.

Visiting Beitin reminded me of my conflicted thoughts of not quite fitting in. When I was growing up in Wisconsin, I was tired of explaining to my non-Arabic-speaking friends that I had been named after my dad's mother, Sadiqa, which means "friend" in Arabic. I wanted a normal name that didn't cause me stress on the first day of school. Would I be called "Sadeek-wa" for the rest of my life? As an adult I would lighten up and laugh at people's witty attempts to blurt out any "s"-sounding names, such as Sequoia, Sasquatch, Sangria, C-3PO, and Somalia.

I miss the relatives I left behind in 1988, but I cherish American ideals. In the United States, I was raised with a different way of perceiving life than my parents were. I was raised to walk on my own yellow brick road. I learned that if I couldn't find one, I should spray-paint my way into happiness and success. And if that didn't work, I could buy yellow shoes.

For me this caused a great deal of confusion regarding how I was supposed to act, behave, feel, and think as a teenager and young adult. Therefore I hid. I wasn't sure what I was hiding from, but I knew I wasn't old enough to be me, even when the law said I was old enough to make wise decisions about who would be President of the United States. But the law of the country is not as strong as the laws of the Hamdan household. "It is simple it is," my dad would say. "If you live under my roof, you live under my rules." There is nothing simple about my dad's rules or his English.

My search for my identity turned into a constant struggle for power. I found strength by walking around in a pair of tight jeans with holes while listening to 1980s hair bands, rock, and hip-hop and applying as much hairspray as the maximum allowed   parts-per-air-I-am-breathing-in   would allow. I answered my parents' requests with "Why?" and "Why not?" I'd ask them, "Why do I have to attend the fifth *henna* party this month?" or "Why can't I wear a tank top in public?" Their response would be the same—"Because." This signaled the end of the discussion, a final decree delivered in one word—a word rarely used to start or end a sentence in any language.

When the fog lifted and I eventually found myself, I decided to fully understand Palestinian women's history and do something meaningful to preserve my heritage. I decided to accept myself and realize that my dual upbringing is a blessing. It isn't that I don't fit in; in fact quite the opposite is true. In addition, traveling to a number of countries in Europe and Brazil in my early twenties for business purposes enabled me to adapt to diverse cultural settings and connect with people from all walks of life.

The other piece to this puzzle is the lack of positive stories surrounding Palestinians—specifically Palestinian women—in Western media. I'm not sure why this is the case, because from my experiences, I know that the culture is rich, engaging, and exotic. Although Palestinian culture, as is the case with most cultures, has its own social issues with which it must contend, I'm accustomed to seeing mainstream media reports on Palestinian women through one lens—one that portrays them as residing in a large, one-size-fits-all, distressed box that is tightly sealed in black duct tape.

A wonderful opportunity presented itself when I was in graduate school in 2011. A loving lady named Sandra Simpson in Tennessee was in the early stages of developing a nonprofit called The Cradleboard Foundation, an organization dedicated to addressing social justice issues through the arts. It was because of her generosity, and the mentorship of a mutual friend, Kate Ransohoff, that I found myself on a plane headed to the West Bank in September 2011. I would be conducting research for my master's thesis, *The Evolution of a Palestinian Woman from 1940 until Now.* During my three-week visit, my first goal was to talk to Palestinian women ages eighteen to ninety about their lives, relationships, education, role models, religion, perceptions regarding their societies, and views of the West. Fifty-five interviews and two hundred cups of mint tea later, I completed the foundation for my thesis. My second goal was to provide a platform to give a voice to Palestinian women. I wanted to provide perspectives on Palestinian women's lives through their eyes.

I then had my master's thesis edited to create this book, which I hope empowers women all over the world, including Palestinians, to take inventory of their lives and find ways in which to create more harmony and balance with themselves and others, within their societies and around the world.

September 2011

Once again I found myself in a modern city built on ancient land. As I made my way from Tel Aviv to Beitin, memories from prior trips flooded my mind. There was the familiarity of palm trees, desert, and uneven mountains that emerged from the red earth. Powerful mountains kept the cities grounded like a paperweights on stacked papers. There were a million and one stones of all shapes and sizes, held together by holy beige-colored sand and faith. However, I didn't recall seeing drivers of BMWs following the same path as donkeys and both complaining of extensive miles, heat, and wear and tear. One could drive for miles on a two-lane highway and see nothing ahead except the same Polaroid shot taken in the rearview mirror.

When I reached Beitin, I was excited at the prospect of seeing my relatives again. It was the same village I'd remembered from the first time I'd stepped foot there twenty-six years before and throughout the years. Beitin, like other Palestinian villages, is shy but full of pride. It clings to its main road like an artery that flows to the heart, unable to survive without it. Like other villages, it has its own story. Beitin has seen more development than one can imagine. As the story goes, Beitin was undeveloped land 180 years ago. Nothing existed then except a natural spring, wild pine trees, thorn bushes, and layers of rock that covered brownish-red dirt. Long ago the inhabitants of Beitin lived in a nearby village called Burqa but relocated to Beitin due to an ongoing tribal feud between two families. The lives of my grandparents' *hamula* (extended family) and other *hamulas* were threatened by this power struggle and moved in the name of peace. Beitin is now known for its olive, fig, almond, and plum trees. Beitin dates back four thousand years and is referred to as "Luz" in the Bible. It is the place where Jacob slept and dreamt of angels ascending and descending a ladder. The followers of Moses call the area Bet El.

During my stay I woke up every morning to the sound of roosters clucking, stray dogs barking, and the first call to prayer—*salat al-fijr,* the dawn prayer. Five times a day, every day, the *imam* at the white brick mosque in the village conducts *adthaan,* a call to prayer, over the loud speaker. It serves as a reminder to Muslims that it is time to pray, to think of and thank God. God is life's guiding compass in Beitin. Sometimes hearing God's name out loud got me out of bed; other times the impending squint of first light lurking behind half-open curtains did the trick. Although people in cities and villages are awake by dawn, the markets don't open until 9:00 a.m.

Methodology and Background

To gain a better understanding of Palestinian women's lives, I frame the conversations in this book into six categories: geography, social class, education, labor market, religion, and nationalism. One is useless without the rest, as they all influence one another. It is like trying to describe an American woman; there are many factors that define an American woman, and Palestinian women are no different. These groupings act as our guide and are not meant to label Palestinian women in any shape or form. These six categories provide context and meaning behind Palestinian women's voices and overall situation, past and present.

Groupings

The women fall into the following age groups. The number of participants is listed for each group.

> Group 1 (ages eighteen to twenty-five) = sixteen
> Group 2 (ages twenty-six to thirty-five) = eight
> Group 3 (ages thirty-six to forty-five) = seven
> Group 4 (ages forty-six to fifty-five) = eleven
> Group 5 (ages fifty-six to seventy-one) = six
> Group 6 (ages seventy-two to ninety) = seven

I chose these age groups mainly to reflect how economic and sociopolitical shifts within Palestinian society affected the women I interviewed. For example women in the seventy-two-to-ninety age group were once young girls who lived in a country called Palestine at that time. They witnessed history in the making when the state of Israel was created in 1948. Other major events that took place during their lifetimes included the 1967 Arab-Israeli War, the 1973 Yom Kippur War, and the *Intifadat* in 1987 and 2000.[9]

Marital Status

Twenty-nine married
Two engaged
Fourteen single
Two divorced
Eight widowed

Education Levels

Twenty-five are enrolled in college or are university
  graduates.
Three earned an associate's degree.
Five earned a master's degree.
Three completed high school.
Eight completed anywhere from seventh to tenth
  grade.
Four completed anywhere from first to sixth
  grade.
Seven received no schooling.

Work

Eleven out of the fifty-five of the women have
  jobs.
Seventeen are looking for work (including
  all females in the eighteen-to-twenty-five
  category).
Twenty-eight are housewives who are not currently
  looking for paid work.

Religious Affiliation

Forty-three Muslims
Seven Christians
Three atheists
Two agnostics

Geography

This study focuses on Palestinian women who were born and raised—or have lived since childhood—in the West Bank. Due to my lack of access to the Gaza Strip, this research unfortunately excludes voices that represent approximately the 838,000 women who live there.[10] Also excluded in this study are Palestinian women in refugee camps and those with Israeli citizenship. However, over the course of three weeks, I was fortunate to interview fifty-five women from the following eighteen West Bank locations.

Beitin	Beit Liqya	Beitunia
Bethlehem	Birzeit	Deir Debwan
Deir Jarir	Jaba	Jeebya
East Jerusalem	Kharbatha al-Misbah	Kufr Ein
Kufr Ni'ma	Nablus	Qibia
Ramallah	Taybeh	Tulkarem

It is also important to explain the identification card system. The Israeli state apparatus requires specific IDs for Palestinian citizens of Israel, Palestinian non-citizens in East Jerusalem, Palestinians in the West Bank, and Palestinians in Gaza. The bureaucracy of Palestinian ID cards since 1948 has made it easier for Israel to discriminate against Palestinians by denoting them as unequal citizens and noncitizens. The ID card system—and to a lesser extent, the permit system—limits Palestinian geographic movement and economic mobility while permitting freer Jewish-Israeli flow and mobility. ID cards demonstrate the power of the Israeli regime to define distinct groups (such as the Palestinians) and bind them to specific territories, while allowing other individuals (Jewish Israelis) to "trespass" over those same boundaries. Through the establishments of ID cards, borders are erected between Jewish and Arab people, not Israeli and Palestinian territory. The ID card system puts into question the nature and territorial boundaries of "Israel" and the geopolitical existence of the "Palestinian territories."

Social Classes

Palestinian social classes from the early 1900s until 1967 fell into four categories: wealthy elite, skilled laborers, farmers, and the landless.

Wealthy elite. This group included returning emigrants, those who were college educated, and those who held important governmental positions.

Members of this class who were born in the villages were still regarded as villagers. They owned land and grew crops like the rest of the villagers but did not till the land on their own. Instead they practiced sharecropping, which allowed other villagers to cultivate their fields in exchange for half of the produce.

Skilled laborers. This group was almost entirely comprised of people who were not directly engaged in agriculture. Included in this class were schoolteachers, village storekeepers, and successful craftsmen such as stonemasons and house builders. Also included in this social class were the few farmers who owned and cultivated enough land so that they became relatively wealthy.

Farmers. This social class, which was by far the largest, was comprised of farmers who owned and cultivated their own land on a small scale. Few of these farmers earned enough from their own land to satisfy their basic needs; therefore they often worked the land of others for a share of the crops or hired themselves out for very modest wages to interested people in—or outside of—the village. Members of this class were constantly in debt to others and from time to time—especially when faced with a drought or when the family had a son who was to be married—found themselves forced to sell a few acres of the little land they owned. By doing this they had to rely more and more upon working for others and therefore lost their prestige and self-respect.

Landless. This group included the elderly who had no one to take care of them, the handicapped, the shiftless, and those who worked as shepherds. With the exception of the latter individuals, members of this class were likely to engage in no regular work of any kind, and almost all of them depended upon charity for their existence.[11]

None of these classes was closed or rigid; it was possible to pass from one class to another.

Although farming dropped considerably since 1967, the rural character of the West Bank is still notable. According to the Palestinian Academic Society for Study of International Affairs (PASSIA):

> There are still around 440 villages ranging in size that form hamlets of a few houses to small towns of up to 20,000 inhabitants. Half the non-camp population is now urban or semi-urban and only 35% rural. Gaza is much more urbanized with only nine villages but large township-like refugee camps. The Nablus region remains predominately rural.

> Among one of the most important changes the Palestinian social structure encountered was the recognition of the role of the Palestinian woman.[12]

What changes have Palestinians, especially Palestinian women, experienced over the last seventy years? Ambition, tradition, technological advances, and unresolved conflict with Israel have created an interesting combination of rules that Palestinian society has followed. Women have an added element of being like fish in search of their own waters to navigate.

Chapter One of this book introduces us to the evolution of Palestinian culture, with a focus on women in the context of communication, the family unit and gender roles, lifestyle, relationships, self-identification, identity within society, role models, and perceptions of the West (primarily of American women). Chapter Two explores current challenges within Palestinian society, while Chapter Three focuses on education and the literacy movement, which perhaps had the greatest effects on altering the course of females' position in Palestinian society. Chapter Four addresses the economic conditions in Palestinian and examines the economic value of a housewife. The ideology and practice of religion in Palestinian society is discussed in Chapter Five, which leads us to taking a deeper look at the *hijab* (the Islamic code of dress); Chapter Six discusses how this code is applied in Palestinian societies and the Arab region as a whole. Chapter Seven is dedicated to the Palestinian costume, the *thoub,* which has served as a means of protecting and portraying the Palestinian heritage and identity of each village, town, and city through visual interpretation. I discuss the lens of national activism and women's roles in politics in Chapter Eight then follow up in Chapter Nine with individual stories of the women I interviewed in order to paint a more vivid picture of the diverseness of Palestinian society. A chapter on research gaps and themes precedes the conclusion, which focuses on the current and future direction of Palestinian women. Where are they headed next?

I hope all women can take the time to observe their history and present situation as a learning tool, and flow with life's currents to create the life they've always imagined for themselves.

"a woman is half of society; she can be anything she wants to be." — Samira, nineteen-year-old Palestinian college student

Chapter One

Society: One Hand Cannot Clap

The Family Unit and Gender Roles

Palestinians were—and still are—a part of a collective society. They believe that "one hand cannot clap" and that lives improve as a result of cooperation and support. Their outlook is similar to the saying "It takes a village to raise a child."

Marriage and the family unit continue to be the focuses of Palestinian culture, but more and more men and women are placing education ahead of saying "I do." It is customary for a woman's brother(s), husband, or father to provide a home and take care of her financial needs. This patriarchal structure relies on the male in the *hamula* (extended family) to financially support his mother, wife, and sister(s) and protect the female's honor and reputation. In the past it was traditional for a Palestinian female to be strictly responsible for raising children, taking care of household affairs, preparing food, cooking, cleaning, and tending the fields.

It wasn't considered common sense for a woman to remain single. It is difficult to say that a married woman at this time could rightly be called a wife or a mother, because she had no choice in deciding whom she could marry, nor could she voice her opinions regarding how to run the household as a married woman. She was a child bearer, and marriage served as a way for her to have children while preserving her honor.

Looking back to when she was fifteen years old in 1955, Um Basil paints this picture for us.

Back then if a woman's husband pissed her off she couldn't say, "Go to hell." She had to put up with him whether she liked it or not. There were instances of divorce back then but not like today. Since a woman wasn't educated and didn't get paid to work, she would have to give up the kids to the father because there was no way to support them.

Lifestyle—A House Without a Woman Is Like a Graveyard[13]

Until the mid-1960s, most Palestinians lived as part of an agricultural collection of *fellaheen* (farmers). People lived off the land's blessings as a way to supplement what little income they could earn in the professional market. Most Palestinians needed to grow what they ate. Eighty-eight-year-old Um Omar says, "Lentils for breakfast, lentils for lunch, and lentils for dinner. That's all we had to eat."

Seventy-one-year-old Um Basil remembers her mother working the fields, but she adds:

The farmer life started phasing out for us. However, I used to walk to the village well to collect water, and that was water for the whole family. We would bathe, drink, wash, and cook with this water every day. We used to put it on our heads and walk back to the house. It wasn't until later in life that we had running water in the house. When I was young, we didn't have electricity—we had to use candles. Only cities had electricity.

The bread was always made homemade. My mom used to do this from scratch—nothing was ready-made back then; everything had to be done by hand. There weren't refrigerators or stoves either. Meat was preserved with salt, and before stoves we used a taboun [clay oven]. We were one of the few families that had a taboun. Everyone else had to cook on an open flame.

"Do you think we could eat cucumbers in the winter?" says Um Hasan, an eighty-five-year-old from a nearby village. "No. And whatever we harvested had to last us until the following harvest. And we were lucky to eat meat during *Eid*."[14]

Um Omar affirms, "Since men worked all day outside the home, we spent all day in the field doing it all. We planted, tilled, harvested, and cooked. Do you think there was a mechanical press back then? No, we had to do it by hand."

And women did so without financial compensation. This is not unique to Palestinians, but it was widespread in what was forming in the third world. We often think of the past romantically, with people living simple lives, but a close examination of past cultures reveals that women often held a subservient relationship to men.[15]

The lack of focus on Palestinian women in society during this timeframe is one of the major reasons that there is very little literature and statistics about them. However, Palestinian culture placed great importance on having women handle domestic affairs. Women were the key element in households in terms of raising children and taking care of all the needs at home.

Women from elite or skilled-labor families, however, historically have played more active roles in society than women from lower classes. Since the early 1900s, these women not only have been interested in—and encouraged—to engage in formal schooling but also have participated in national agendas and the advancement of women's roles in society.

Over time the roles of Palestinian women expanded within marriage and outside the home. Several factors contribute to this expansion, but it mainly stems from the shift in perception regarding education and the need to provide for families during active conflict. The fifty-five Palestinian women I interviewed believe females' positions in society fall into one of the following seven categories.

1. **Inside the home**. "All things related to the house, kids, cooking, and everything related to that inside the home," says Talia, a sixty-two-year-old mother of four with a first-grade education. Five of the women I interviewed expressed the same sentiment—mainly uneducated older women from villages. It would be misleading to say that a rural life combined with age and lack of education are the sole reasons these women hold these beliefs, but this is generally the rule. In contrast, my eighty-six-year-old grandmother, who has no education and lived most of her life in the village, says that a woman can do anything she wants to do in life. She is, perhaps, one of the exceptions to the rule.

2. **Inside the home and in professional fields.** "Today's woman is a nurse, doctor or lawyer and she's the one who still has to take care of house work and raise the kids," says sixty-two-year-old Suhad. Three women expressed the same belief.

3. **All parts of society or anything she chooses.** Thirty-six women stated this opinion. Mariam is an urban twenty-seven-year-old mother of two who earned her master's degree before getting married. She works at a media company and is straightforward in saying:

The roles aren't different for a Palestinian man or woman. In life and life's demands, we find that a woman can live with or without a man. She can do all the things that a man does and more—working and taking care of her household. Today's woman has two roles; she brings in money like a man and makes decisions like a man. The "soldier" way of life is no longer inside the house—there are only soldiers outside.

My husband and I both work, and we both make decisions regarding the house and our desires. If the house requires someone to watch the kids because I have a professional or personal evening appointment, then my husband will watch the kids. He has no problems with it.

4. **Equal to a man.** Women like Samira, a third-year college student, believe "a woman is half of society." Five women fall into this category.

5. **Education.** Fifty-eight-year-old Lina, who earned a degree in education, believes a Palestinian woman "can be anything she wants to be, as long as she's educated and can take care of herself. She can choose when she wants to get married." This is the message Lina has been teaching her seventeen- and nineteen-year-old daughters since they were little girls. Ten women agree. Although most of women I spoke to are pro-education, these ten women specifically centered their responses around education.

Aisha, a thirty-year-old mother of four, gives a unique response regarding education. It is a statement of nationalism. She was still a student at Birzeit University when she became pregnant with her first child. The remarkable part of her story is that she completed her college education in between giving birth to three children. Her parents and in-laws took care of the kids while she studied. She is now pregnant with her fifth child and would like to go back to teaching when all the children are in school. Aisha says:

> The Palestinian woman has a role to educate herself and children and remind them of where they came from. Because of the Israeli occupation, we have a duty to fight for our land. We have to fight for our lives. Otherwise our children won't have anywhere to live when they grow up. [16]

I discuss education and nationalism in more detail later in the book, but it's important to realize that education has changed the lives of women around the world, including Palestinian women. Nationalism is also a very important part of the Palestinian narrative. The conflict with Israel has pushed Palestinian women outside of their traditional roles.

6. **No role in society without her husband.** Two women believe this, including eighty-eight-year-old Um Amjad, who says:

> A woman like me, whose husband died a long time ago, does not have much of a role in society. What can a woman do without her husband or a man to help take care of things? When her husband dies, so does the woman's respect.

Women who are Um Amjad's age were brought up to believe that it is a husband's job to take care of all financial responsibilities. They believe that the self-worth of a woman is tied to what a man can offer her, rather than believing they can provide for and support themselves.

7. **Conscience of society.** Rania, a former activist, educator, and music enthusiast, tells us:

> Women should be the conscience of any society. Women have always been, maybe because of their motherly natures, much more willing to sacrifice and have peace in the family. Being a mother means you know that injustice is one of the worst basic causes for conflict. You know not to be unjust in the family, or discriminate between one child and the other. When you teach a child justice, the child will grow up to be just. Women know this by experience, not by birth. They are the moderators and have to keep the balance in the family.

Indeed, growing up in a Palestinian household and having a large extended family, I was surrounded by women who spoke their minds. It is the women who plan, organize, and implement social gatherings and weddings and who hold families together. Socialization, community celebration, mourning, and sharing are common traits that flow throughout Palestinian and Middle Eastern societies. These traits allow for learning about everyday life lessons and also the preservation of heritage. In my opinion, Palestinian men have equally important roles but have been raised to feel they are more deserving than women. Men are raised to seek prestige and power, whereas women are now raised to be smart, graceful, and nurturing.

I'm very happy to hear that Palestinian women have a positive self-perception. I know it can be hard to stay positive when parts of society do not fully appreciate the social capital women have within the culture. It is also difficult to see women who speak of individuality but do not lead by example.

This brings us to two important questions. First, is it important for a Palestinian woman to have a man in her life? Second, which women served as role models to Palestinian women during their upbringing?

Relationships—Is It Important to Have a Man in Your Life?

A common misperception about Palestinian and Middle Eastern societies is that a woman has no choice regarding whom she marries and when she marries. Furthermore many people believe that the option of being single is, well, not an option. This is not true either.

According to Islam and Christianity, a woman has the right to choose and refuse marriage proposals. Culturally the patriarchal structure remains intact to this day in conservative countries such as Saudi Arabia, which is a Muslim country. The male patriarchy system is applicable to both Palestinian

Muslim and Christian societies, but it's less restrictive or widely implemented in Christian families.

The patriarchal structure is one ingredient that jibes with conservative to liberal interpretations of religion and is grounded with what is culturally acceptable. A family in Jerusalem functions very differently than a family in Saudi Arabia, even if they are both considered equally religious. The same applies to villages, towns, and cities within a country or region. Thus what is culturally or religiously acceptable in Jerusalem is not the same as what is acceptable in the Palestinian village of Beit Liqya.

To the West this sounds nothing short of confusing. It's like ordering Turkish coffee and not knowing how strong, sweet, bitter, light, or dark it will be. There are many versions of coffee in the Middle East, depending on its origin. Each batch creates its own flavor. While this may not be detrimental in the world of coffee beans, it has caused a great deal of confusion surrounding women's rights in Arab and Muslim-majority countries. However, I view this model no differently than that of US culture. Each person's interpretation of religion varies. What is acceptable to one conservative Christian may not be the case with another equally conservative Christian from the same denomination. It depends on social class, economic background, education levels, and personal life experiences.

When I asked the question, "Is it important to have a man in your life?" several groups and subgroups of answers emerged. Relationships, it turns out, fall into several categories, including "nice," "a matter of choice," or "not important at all." These were straightforward answers. Other women believe relationships are "very important" or "important," but for some it's putting the cart before the horse—there are conditions or reasons for being in a relationship. Let's explore their answers in more depth.

1. **Very important or important.** Seventy-one-year-old Um Basil says:

> *Yes. It's very important. If I didn't get married, I'd be eating, drinking, and living with my parents for as long as they are alive. Life is about family. Otherwise you'll wake up at the age of forty and wonder what you have in your life...nothing. For us [Palestinians] a man is himaaya [protection] for the woman. He works and takes cares of the family. I don't have to worry about how am I going to pay the bills. I play an important and equally supportive role, but it's inside the home.*

Um Basil, however, believes that times have changed because women are educated and fully capable of working outside the home while being in a relationship. She is a very nurturing and straightforward person. While I understand her logic, in the back of my mind, I wonder why she could not project a different outcome for her life as a single person. Again it tells me how deeply rooted certain traditions are in Palestine and the Arab region.

Twenty-eight women agree that relationships are important or very important, but two subthemes emerged.

1a. **Finding the right person is key.** Eight women believe relationships are important or very important, as long as you can find the right person.

1b. **Education comes first.** Hiba is a twenty-year-old law student who says, "Relationships are important, but a woman shouldn't be in one unless she's educated and can stand on her own two feet." Seven women fall into this category.

2. **Personal Choice.** Five women straightforwardly say, "It's a personal matter."

3. **Not important at all.** "Unless a woman wants to have children," says thirty-year-old Yasmine, "then a relationship isn't important. A woman can take care of herself." A total of eleven women believe a relationship isn't important. Surprisingly a few married women fall into this category. One married woman was open enough to comment further. Hanan is forty-five years old and has a fifth-grade education. She and her husband have three children and have been married for twenty-seven years, but their marriage turned sour. She says:

> The man whom I call "husband" doesn't really do anything. He sleeps a lot and doesn't interact or get to know me. I was forced to sell the gold from my wedding for him to remarry a woman. But if I leave, I end up

losing my kids. I'm unwilling to do that. I would rather be miserable at home than leave my kids.

We were married twenty-four years before he remarried.[17] He waited until I went through menopause as an excuse for him to say he wanted more kids. What he really wanted was an Israeli ID card and married an Arab woman in Israel. She comes by the house once or twice a week. But she isn't the problem—he is the problem for marrying her. The ironic thing is that they cannot have kids. It is great that God cut off his prosperity [rizeq] just like he cut off mine. He fell from my eye when he got married again.

4. **No response.** Ten women from various age groups did not answer the question. I'm not sure whether they felt uncomfortable voicing their opinions or have no opinion regarding relationships. Some of these women may have hidden their feelings, which is a topic to explore further in future studies.

Most of the Palestinian women who participated in this study state that they are not interested in being in a relationship just for the sake of being in one. Women understand that by delaying marriage for the sake of education they are in a better position to make decisions about their future.

Role Models: It Takes a Village to Raise Social Consciousness

Another important question is, "Which women served as role models to you during their upbringing?"

"No one really," says thirty-five-year-old Suhad. "I just want to be a better person, not really wishing I could be like someone else." Forty-five out of fifty-five women answered along the same lines.

Almost every Palestinian woman I spoke with has a different perception regarding what constitutes a role model. Unlike in the United States, where athletes, leaders, actresses, actors, celebrities, and successful businessmen and women are considered role models, Palestinian women aspire to be like other women who are doing good deeds in their communities; they have a very difficult time singling out one woman. The term "role model" does not have the same weight in Palestinian societies as it does in the United States and other Western countries. The concept of a role model almost seems foreign to Palestinian women of all ages. They perceive it as an unusual question, perhaps because Muslims are not supposed to idolize individuals.[18]

However, most Palestinian Muslims, Christians, atheists, and agnostics in this study feel the same about the concept of a role model, which would make us believe this fact is linked to an ideology of culture rather than faith.

One interesting response regarding role models came from a twenty-five-year-old college graduate named Ameera. She explains:

There was an American woman who came to this village and loved it here so much that she came back with her husband. She comes and goes between the United

States and Palestine. She is educated and loves helping our community. She's a doctor who always has a positive attitude—and even though she has a lot of money, it's how she socializes and interacts with our community that makes her a good role model.

Perhaps the most inspiring response to this question came from a forty-two-year-old mother of three who completed a fourth-grade education. It shows us how far women have come to believe in the importance of education.

No one famous, but I look up to women in our society who are educated. I can't read or write, but I learned how to sew. I would like to learn to read and write in order to be a better person.When I grew up, society did not care about education. I stopped going to school after fourth grade for a reason. I was the only person in the family who could take care of the household chores after my mother gave birth to my younger sister. My brothers worked outside the house to feed their own families. My father was not financially taking care of us. Palestinians and my parents at that time didn't think of the future—how important it would be for me to stay in school. Right now I don't have to go back to an institution to learn but want to be able to read and write.

I have not yet discussed education in depth, but in my opinion, education singlehandedly has altered the course of Palestinian women's positions in society.

Society's Perception of Palestinian Women

Although most of the Palestinian women in this study perceive themselves to be equal to men, they don't believe society sees them in the same way. One limitation to this study is the lack of discussion with Palestinian men regarding their thoughts about Palestinian women. When Palestinian women are asked, "What would you change about how society views women?" there is no simple answer. In fact there are many responses, including the action words "allow," "remove," and "give" or words of empowerment, such as "choice," "freedom," "rights," "appreciation," and "respect. These words are interdependent, with references to both education and empowerment.

1. **Allow: education, personal decisions and choices.** Rania wants society to "allow women to make decisions without 'group think' or permission from family members." Indeed, despite the number of women who are more educated than men, deeply rooted traditions are not easy to break. Society as a whole includes women, many of whom have been raised to prioritize family over individuality.

Fatimeh, a fifty-three-year-old widow with nine educated children, wishes that "society would allow a woman to complete her education and support her decision to be self-sufficient."

2. **Remove: restrictions, rules, and gender inequalities.** Seven women agree that society should

remove rules and restrictions regarding how women should live their lives.

Thirty-year-old college educated Aisha wants to change the limited perception of a woman's role in society. She says she wants to do away with the notion "that all she's good for is getting married and having kids. We have women in higher power and have shown that we are capable of doing more than raising kids in life. Our opinions and advice are valuable for raising the status of the society as a whole."

3. **Give: freedom, rights, respect, and appreciation.** Thirty-three-year-old Dalia was born and raised in East Jerusalem. She wants "society to have a greater appreciation for a woman's opinion and give her more power and authority in life's decisions."

Hayat is a mature twenty-one year-old law student who agrees with Dalia and directs her message to Palestinian women.

I wish society could see the good that women are contributing to their communities. I wish every woman could see the importance of education and how it's changing the world. By educating herself, she creates awareness for other women in society to raise their own value.

A sixty-two-year-old divorced mother of four who earned a college degree and has been an educator for more than thirty years says:

I wish society would be more supportive of women's rights. Religion gave the woman a great deal of rights—how to be treated by her parents and her husband—but because of our customs, society tries to shame the woman into saying and doing things she shouldn't. For example a woman is supposed to receive her share of land when her father passes away, but in the past, society tried to shame her into not taking her share by saying things like, "What's more important to you—giving your share to your brothers or the money?" Today parents give equal shares to their daughters and sons without giving their daughters any guilt.

The number of strong women I met impressed me, but I feel they need much more support to fully live up to their potential. Despite the socioeconomic and political challenges, women are still pushing forward toward their goals.

Self-Identity—Tied and Untied to Self

A common misperception is that a woman in the Arab region is tied to her husband and cannot voice her opinion regarding the relationship. Although Palestinians are part of a collective society, most of women I spoke with believe in the importance of establishing their own identities. When I asked them, "How important is it for a Palestinian woman to have her own identity, separate from society and her husband?" only seven women said they believe it's better to be tied to a man. *"Marboota"* means "tie" in Arabic and is commonly used to describes relationships. In the Arab region, the word *"marboota"* often means being committed or connected to a relationship, individual, job, project, or school, rather than being tied down.

"Self-identity," says eighty-five-year-old Um Nasser, "is very important. Without herself she can't be self-sufficient. It's not good to depend on someone else for your happiness." Thirty-nine out of the fifty-five Palestinian women I interviewed agree with Um Nasser and say self-identity is **important** or **very important**.

What I gathered from my conversations is the recognition of the connection between self-identify and self-empowerment. "A woman needs to empower herself and not let anyone bring her down," explains fifty-three-year-old Soraya.

1. **Self-identity means balancing self, society, and spouse.** What I find intriguing are the six women who gave similar responses to that of Um Mustafa, a forty-three-year-old mother of four, who says, "It's important for a Palestinian woman to have her own identity, as long as it does not affect the relationship between her and her husband. A woman is part of society. Palestinians are a collective people whose values are based on the family." This brings in the idea of balance, which is something we have not heard yet in this research. As I was raised in the United States, the concepts of self-identity, balance, and achievement are ingrained into my mind, and I find ways to maintain this equilibrium. Although family is important in American culture, I believe

the individual and his or her rights are valued more than collective welfare.

2. **Self-identity is not important.** Not all women agree with Um Mustafa. Seven women think self-identity is not important at all. Amal is forty-one years old and thinks a woman "should not have her own identity. She should be tied to a man because it makes her stronger. There are things a woman can't do on her own that only a man can do."

I expected older women to say something along these lines but wasn't prepared to hear it from younger women. One could say Amal's lack of education is the reason, but we just heard Um Nasser, an eighty-five-year-old woman with no education, discuss the importance of independence. I'm not sure what to make of these statements except that a woman's background and life experiences make her who she is.

Cross-Cultural Review: Are There Similarities Between Palestinian and American Women?

Do many Palestinian women believe there are similarities and differences between Palestinian and American women? The answer is yes to both. However, many of the women I spoke with do not have an opinion on the subject or did not have enough knowledge to answer this question. Twenty-six women did not respond or said they weren't sure. I feel that their lack of interaction with American women and/or media images is the reason behind these responses.

1. **Biology.** Fifty-year-old Alia, who is educated, believes "a woman is a woman, regardless of where she's from." Six other women agree.

2. **Career focused, with family balance.** Ameena is sixty-two years old and college educated. She believes American and Palestinian women's priorities are similar. "Both want to be successful, with careers, family, and kids." A total of five women responded along these lines.

3. **Education focused.** "We're both focused on education, education, education. It is the key to creating more balance in our lives," says twenty-nine-year-old Khadeejah. Three women fall into this category.

4. **Struggling for equality in the workplace and society.** Fourth-year college student Zahra says, "Both are women and dream to be part of society. I imagine that every woman dreams of this in every society." Five women feel the same way.

Thirty-year-old Jumana says, "Women are the same all over the world. Everyone is looking for financial and emotional security."

Maysa is the director of a private school in Ramallah. She states, "American and Palestinian women struggle for gender equality and to get value from male colleagues, brothers, and fathers. It is just worse in some Palestinian areas than in the United States. But women are subjected to violence all over the world, and Palestinian women are not immune to it."

It is a common perception that Palestinian women live in abusive relationships. While it's true that approximately 37 percent of married Palestinian women in Gaza and the West Bank experienced physical or emotional violence in 2012, women in American society also face high rates of violence. These statistics within Palestinian society are hard to explain because Palestinian men and women live in a culture that has experienced violence from within and outside of society for the past four generations. When you combine national conflict with high unemployment rates in a society where men are supposed to be the breadwinners in the family, the men are more likely to take out their frustrations inside the home.

Maysa articulates it on a more personal level for us:

> I've read reports where women all over the world are subjected to domestic violence—it's horrific. You find it everywhere. Honor killings and whatnot is all very disturbing, but still it doesn't mean that American women aren't facing similar problems in certain cultures. It's not spoken of very openly. You don't know what's behind closed doors. I know of few reports and studies that indicate when economic and political situations are very difficult in Palestine men become frustrated. They can't provide for their families. They can't work. They can't put food on the table. And in our society, the male's role is to do just that. Then he goes home and has six kids to feed after working long hours [with] little pay, if any. If he has to take his stress out on someone; it gets taken

out on his wife. All of that—coupled with what comes from the Israeli occupation, stress, and agony—translates into abuse toward women.

I know there's an indirect link between occupation and violence. You see people going about their normal business, but you don't know what's going on behind the scenes. They probably lived a childhood that has seen a lot of violence or violation. "Can't go here. Can't go there." They see their parents spoken to very roughly by a seventeen-year-old Israeli soldier. All of this impacts children and caries through into adulthood.

Here I am, a forty-five-year-old, and have lived here most of my life. I lived through the occupation since I was two years old. I lived through the first Intifadah, second Intifadah, and regional conflict. Have all these experiences throughout my life changed my personality? I'm sure, no doubt. There's a lot of hidden stuff that's hard to unpack.

In the United States, if a woman or man experiences anything traumatic, they automatically see a therapist and make it sound like the problems stem from their childhood and relationship with their father or mother. Americans spend all this money trying to unpack what is causing them pain—to unravel how their childhood impacted their relationships as adults, with their spouse, kids, peer, and wives. For Palestinians it's the whole society. The entire population has been subjected to so many traumas. How do you think that affects us as human beings? Our relationships? How am I raising my kids differently because of what I went through? How is my relationship with my husband altered because of what I went through?

49

Furthermore, there is a high rate of depression amongst the Palestinians, which does not help in solving the issue of domestic violence. Forbes published an article on February 27, 2013 entitled *A Young Doctor Fights the Depression Epidemic in Palestine* and states that "forty percent of Palestinians are clinically depressed, a rate unmatched anywhere in the world. It's more than triple in the U.S., ten times higher than the U.K. and four to eight times higher than in Scandinavia, where the sun doesn't shine for a good part of the year."[19]

5. **Family focused, wanting to raise good children and healthy families.** Twenty-seven year-old Mariam believes "an American mother wants to take care of her kids like a Palestinian woman." Agreeing with Mariam, Alia says, "They are both interested in raising their children with morals." Five women fall into this category.

American and Palestinian Differences

Many of the perceived differences Palestinian women cite are positive. Palestinian women view American women as self-empowered individuals who are able to change their circumstances and do not need permission from men. However, Palestinian women also believe American women are still struggling for equality, like women all over the world, and do not know what it's like to live under occupation. Thirty-four women did not respond to the question regarding identifying differences between American and Palestinian women. This is a very high non-response rate. Again I believe this is due to the lack of face-to-face interaction with American women, and perhaps Palestinian women do not want to articulate false or biased statements. Five themes emerged from the women who did answer.

1. **Cultural norms.** The answers in this category pertain to differences in fashion, how women and children are raised in society, and thought processes. When it comes to cultural norms, seventeen Palestinian women state they believe Arab women and communities are connected all the time while American women are raised as individuals. Nadia says:

> *The American woman leaves the house at eighteen years old. The Palestinian woman stays at home until she gets married. An American woman is allowed to have kids without getting married. A Palestinian can't take trips on her own like the boys. In America a woman can come and go as she pleases. But for us it's also a problem when girls can't leave their village to study. I'm fortunate because I'm a daughter from a village, and as a law student, I've been able to travel to Norway, Germany, Turkey, Qatar, and Morocco. It all depends on how open your parents are.*

There's also a "difference in how Palestinian and American women are taught to think. It's instilled in us since birth," says Mariam.

Thirty-five-year-old Naeema uses money to illustrate a point. "American women use their money differently than Palestinian women. Americans' lives start at retirement—they travel, relax, and enjoy life. Palestinians save all their money and apply it toward expanding their homes."

Nadine, mother of three, agrees:

It's not that one way of thinking is better than the other; it's just a difference in how we perceive life. A Palestinian woman who reaches the age of sixty thinks that's it—she's done with life and will be financially supported by her family. She sits at home and does nothing. American women are different—it's like their life is just beginning. American women who are fifty-five to sixty-five years old look for more opportunities to explore and also have energy and curiosity for life.

Thirty-year-old Amira echoes Nadine's thoughts:

Whatever situation a Palestinian woman falls into—if she is twenty [years old] and her husband passes away, that's it. A woman will accept this fate and not do anything to better herself. It's like time stops, and she stays in this moment of feeling down for herself or thinking she has to marry someone much older than her to continue receiving financial support.

Americans have something inside of them that's not inside of us. I don't know what the word is for it. Americans will save money to be able to sightsee. We save money to add on to the house or marry our sons and daughters. That's it. We don't save money to see the world. We save money for our kids and grandkids, not for us.

2. **Gender relations.** Nine Palestinian women think American women do not prioritize a man's needs over their own. "They don't put men first in their lives like Palestinian women do," says Samira, a first-year college student.

Eighty-eight-year-old Um Basil has a different perspective.

> *American women are great role models. They stand up for themselves and do something regardless if a man wants them to or not. At the same time, though, they may be sacrificing a relationship for power and trying to do things on their own, like raise children. This is not a good thing. Children need a man and a woman figure in their life. Women can't do it all by themselves. But here we try to rely on the man to provide us everything, and that is not a good thing either.*

3. **Rights.** Twelve women believe American women fight for their rights more than Palestinian women and overall have a greater degree of equality in society.

Raeda is fifty-five years old and single. She never married but put her life into her work as an educator. She says:

An American woman has more equality and receives fifty percent of her husband's net worth; we have not reached that level yet. We don't have the same respect as an American woman. Although they are similar to Palestinians and face abusive relationships, American women are more likely to demand their rights. Palestinians are culturally more open than other countries in the Middle East, but the men are still assertive and have leverage over women here.

Ghada is a sixty-two-year-old divorced mother of one. She believes "American women have their freedoms and can do whatever they want, regardless of whether a man says yes or no. This is something we hope to aspire to have here—more voice in society."

4. **Self-perception:** Three women (ages twenty-four, thirty-seven, and fifty-three) are straightforward in saying, "American women have more self-confidence."

5. **Israeli occupation.** Twenty-one-year-old Sabina says, "There's a big difference between how we *want* to live our lives versus how we *have* to live our lives."

Nabiha, a retired educator, remarks:

I do not believe an American woman can understand what it's like to live like a Palestinian woman, whose children have gone to jail for no reason and can't be seen for years. We live a very hard life, and no one can understand the Palestinian life. An American woman doesn't know what it's like to have her house bulldozed or live under occupation.

Overall I was pleased that Palestinian women perceive American women in a positive light. The lack of responses concerns me, however, and I hope the future brings more cross-cultural interaction between American and Palestinian women.

This chapter highlights the richness and diversity of Palestinian women's thoughts regarding society and themselves. Palestinian women acknowledge their self-worth, but many must fight to maintain their value. Even from the small sample of my interviews with fifty-five women, we learn that there is no "one-size-fits-all" Palestinian woman. Their challenges are to find balance with respect to society's traditional rules, while being who they are as individuals and collectively working to establish autonomy as a nation. I discuss this in more detail in the next chapter.

Chapter Two

Challenges: Rising Above Limitations, Expectations, and Conditions

"I complained because I had no shoes until I met a man who had no feet."
                                        —*Arab proverb*

"Know the well and its lid," eighty-eight-year-old Um Omar says. This is a common proverb and serves as reminder regarding the importance of understanding a situation very well. "With this knowledge," she continues, "anyone can handle the challenges associated with it."

Palestinian women face many challenges, ones shared by women around the world. In this chapter, women voice their opinions regarding six issues that present challenges in their lives.

1. **Lack of rights, freedom, and support.** This covers everything from society's social traditions (eleven women), restrictions and rules (ten), lack of respect (three), education (two), equality (one), and male dominance (two). There is also a lack of support for widows (two), older women (one), women juggling home and professional life (two), and women in general (two).

Eighty-five-year-old Um Rami says, "Life is hard all around, but I would say the challenge is not being valued for our experiences and wisdom." She's had no schooling and raised four children who've become high school or college educated.

Nineteen year-old Samira has an equally powerful message. She says:

> Society doesn't walk in my shoes and can't speak on behalf of me. I can raise my voice and be heard when I want to be heard. Life is no one's business but yours. Inside our souls, we as women can be free. Until we free ourselves from ourselves, then we will continue to be slaves in our own society.

Maysa is a forty-five-year-old private school director with a master's degree. She believes women are also part of the problem.

> [There is] inequality and the continued perception by society and by women that our main role is to be

child bearers and wives. I think the self-perception of a woman is not where it should be. We need to believe more in our potential as human beings who are able to give back to society in productive ways. Women aren't raised with that notion. Instead it's along the lines of "You are a woman, and you will grow up, get married, have kids." Very few women are raised on the notion that they are going to grow up, get a great education and career, and do wonderful things with their life. Very few women have that viewpoint. They are an obstacle in their own development.

Aziza is a twenty-one-year-old undergrad student who says:

In order for a Palestinian woman to have more in life financially or whatever she wants to do in life, she cannot neglect her role and duties at the house. In fact she has to do double work. Why doesn't the man feel it's his place to do household chores? If it's a choice between work and house, then house comes first. Another challenge is that a woman always has to take permission from her parents and eventually from her husband. Also she can't live on her own.

We find this is often the case for women in other emerging countries, such as India and Brazil.

2. **Lack of work.** Eleven women feel, for various reasons, that not working keeps them from being able to raise their status in society. It is traditional for single women to live at home until they marry. Working single women often use their paychecks to

supplement the family income rather than taking care of themselves. I explore the Palestinian economy in greater depth later in the book to provide a better understanding of its complexity, but national conflict, traditions, and lack of support (e.g., childcare and transportation) are three major reasons that prevent women from entering the labor market.

Twenty-five-year-old Bethlehem native Aziza says, "Because of the Israeli occupation, we can't come and go as we please. We can't enter Israel to work without a permit."

Um Mohamed is fifty-three years old and has four children. She became a widow at a young age and worked as a house cleaner in Israel for twenty-five years to put food on the table. But five years ago, the Israeli government decided to punish the residents of her village by no longer issuing work permits. She has zero schooling, and it's difficult for her to find any other type of work. She says:

> There are days when a woman without a husband doesn't see a shekel. When a person does find work, you have to work for eight hundred to one thousand shekels (two hundred fifty to three hundred fifty dollars) a month and extremely long hours. Well, that's slave work, and it doesn't pay the bills. You have to be able to sleep and relax. At least back in the day, women could find food without having to buy it. Now life is more difficult.

Lara is thirty-three years old and has a bachelor's degree in education but knows how difficult it can be to find a job. With unemployment in the West Bank as high as 23 percent, and 38 percent in Gaza, connections are very important. She says, "We can't find jobs, and there is no money to get into higher education. There is no such thing as student loans."

I've heard this story too many times during my family visits to the West Bank. Many mothers who are interested in completing their education as adults are unable to, unless they can pay each semester's tuition at the beginning of the semester. To do that they have to be able to work, and to work in the West Bank, one must have a degree, be part of a thriving family business, or have really great connections. Unless a woman has a strong family to support her, she will have a harder time turning this dream into a reality.

There are fewer options for Palestinians to attend college than in the West. It's not necessarily true that "there is no such thing as student loans," but they are difficult to obtain. The Ministry of Education, universities, and volunteer organizations provide loans and assistance to those who excel in school or fit specific requirements.

What we don't hear in the news, however, is that Palestinians have managed to educate themselves because they live collectively. If a father and his two boys are working, the money goes into the "pot" for the entire family, with each making some sort of sacrifice to support the other. A brother may have to do with a little less for a few years while his sister is in school. When she graduates, however, she'll have an opportunity to work and support the family too. I see it as a catch-22, because to some degree, no one in society is able to fully live up to his or her potential alone; there is a great deal of interdependency in Palestinian society due to the societal, political, and economical systems in place.

3. **National liberation**. Seven women cited the Palestinian-Israeli conflict as a crippling factor in their lives. Fifty-three-year-old research director Samar believes the issues Palestinian women deal with are layered. She says:

> There are different levels of challenges. First of all the occupation is a big challenge because it places restrictions on mobility. It's further marginalizing women because they can't go through the mountains and travel the rocky roads by foot. The political conflict causes a second challenging layer because it is also reflected within the family itself (i.e., the kids or husbands [being] in jail). This affects women's careers and cripples them from being able to take care of their family.

4. **Everything**. Eight women say there are many challenges or that everything in life is a challenge.

5. **Religion**. Thirty-five-year-old Samya is a second wife, originally from the Nablus area and now living in a village near Ramallah. She completed high school and never was married prior to this relationship. She is attractive and smart and cannot understand why she succumbed to being a second wife. She eventually told me her story, and I learned that she comes from

a very poor family and did not leave the house so that she could take care of her ill mother.

Samya was thirty years old when her mother passed away, and she married two years later. By that time she was considered an old bride-to-be by her village's standards and thought her only option was to marry an older man or become a second wife. Unfortunately Samya grew up with that idea and didn't think she could have more for herself in life. Samya believes one of society's biggest challenges is the interpretation of religion, which affects everything else in a person's life. She says, "A Palestinian woman is tied to her father's decisions. Then she's tied to her husband's decisions. Religion gave women freedom that has not been translated well by society."

6. **Education.** "Lack of proper education is an issue," says seventy-nine-year-old Rania. She continues:

> *In other words learning to be open, tolerant, [with a] flexible brain and basing your judgment on authentic information—not, "I heard someone on the radio say this" or whatever is read on the Internet. Another big challenge is "What does religion mean to a woman?" Is it the outward dress? Is this religion to women? Is it what man imposes on you? Women have not fully defined what religion means to them. Many women follow rules rather than ask questions and create their own beliefs and values.*

Despite the long list of challenges Palestinians face, one thing is for certain—character elements of will, determination, pride, and personal faith have supported Palestinian women in their attempts to make the best out of their situations. They understand that resistance and self-determination come in many forms, which the naked eye may not always see. Not every Palestinian woman will challenge society's rules, but they all rely on the strength of others to brighten the road for them. Many Palestinian women understand that circumstances change over time, not overnight. This brings us to the next major topic of interest, which was a major turning point in the advancement of Palestinian women's positions in society—education as a vehicle for social capital.

Chapter Three

Education: The Cheapest Pen is Better than Memory

One day I received a lead to interview a seventy-one-year-old mother of eight children, Um Basil. I sat in her guest room with my notebook and digital recorder in hand, patiently waiting for her to finish her noontime prayer. She turned out to be a very direct and has a worldly sense to her. She offered me hot tea with mint before we began. A mother to eight children, she understands life has handed her more opportunities than women received in her mother's generation. She calmly explains:

> *Women my mom's age did not go to school. They received zero education—more like "zero minus." Marriage was more important, and parents may not have been able to*

*buy notebooks and books to be able to send their kids
to school. Villages only offered education to a certain
level (fourth, fifth, sixth grade), and if you wanted a
higher education, you had to send your kids to a city
like Ramallah or al-Bireh. Men could not afford to
send all their kids to the city every day. Women did not
traditionally leave the house, so it was hard for them to
let their daughters travel alone to a city. There was also
no point in sending girls to school, because there were
no jobs that supported women in the marketplace. It
was also shameful for women to work outside the house.*

Very few Palestinians could read or write prior to
the 1940s, as most Palestinians were *fallaheen* (farmers), and this lifestyle did not require a textbook education. In fact it was almost unheard of for a woman
to have any schooling. The exception to this rule were
women born into wealthy and skilled families who
valued education and could afford to pay for their
children's schooling. These women not only became
educated but also participated in social development
and community issues. Overall Palestinians believe
that in the absence of what books can teach them in
school, learning is possible through socialization.

Fifty-three-year-old Fatimeh wishes she had completed high school. Instead she married at age fifteen
and had nine children. Unfortunately she became a
widow at age forty-five and has no way of getting
a job with her lack of education and the current
depressed economy. The money she was left with
after her husband's death will last only a few more
years, but her older children are highly educated and

will support her for the rest of her life. As much as she values education, Fatimeh also understands the power of social learning in Palestinian communities. She says:

> Uneducated Palestinian women have been able to learn how to do things in life and, to some degree, make better decisions than they would have made on their own, because of how much they socialize with others. So an uneducated person learns a lot of life's lessons and about the outside work through interaction. Groups of women learn from each other. You don't need a formal education for everything. Life is an education lesson.

When Palestine was under British rule (1918–1947), the number of females attending elementary schools increased absolutely and relatively to the number of boys in elementary schools. The number of girls in school, however, never rose above 23 percent of the total Palestinian enrollment in elementary schools. At the secondary level, their percentage was much lower; the educational opportunities for girls in rural areas were always minimal.[20]

In his diaries Humphrey Bowman, British Director of Education from 1920 to 1936, reflects on the Palestinian emphasis of educating Arab girls in domestic skills over book learning. Educating girls was not a high priority. He writes:

> The British believed that the majority of girls did not need more than an elementary education, with most urban girls' schools offering six or

seven years of schooling. The only public secondary school for girls was the Women's Teachers'
College, which accepted a small number of
pupils each year. The British repeatedly claimed
that they could not expand girls' education
because of the lack of Muslim female teachers.

When the number of Muslim women entering
the profession increased, the British were unable
to increase the number of available posts because
of budgetary considerations. The British also dif-
ferentiated between urban and rural girls' education. Village girls' schools formed a small percentage of all village schools, and offered at most
only four years of primary education, as opposed
to six or seven. Top pupils in village schools were
invited to attend the Women's Rural Teachers'
Training Center in Ramallah, where they studied elementary-school subjects in addition to
simple pedagogy, domestic science, and agricultural skills. Its opening in 1935, seventeen years
after the establishment of the Department of
Education, also manifests the girls' education in
the villages.[21]

After 1948 the number of girls enrolled in
school increased, although the institution largely
responsible for the growth in female enrollment
was the United Nations Relief and Works Agency
(UNRWA)—that is to say, a non-Palestinian agency
set up by the United Nations to care for Palestinian
refugees. UNRWA apparently readdressed the imbal-
ance to the point where female-to-male enrollment

showed a ratio of 74:100 in 1961 in the Gaza Strip, and 75:100 in 1967 in the West Bank; the ratios have continued to even out up until the present day. By 1990–1991, females made up 47.2 percent of primary-level students in government schools in the West Bank (excluding Jerusalem) and 48.3 percent in UNRWA schools in the Gaza Strip. These figure correspond roughly to the percentage of females age five to nineteen in the population of the occupied territories in 1989 (48 percent).[22]

According to the Palestinian Central Bureau of Statistics (PCBS), more than 85,000 males and 109,000 females were enrolled in a university or community college in the 2009–2010 school year. Five years earlier (2004–2005), only 18,000 males and 15,600 females attended a university or community college.[23] Given that the Palestinian national literacy rate is 94 percent, this speaks volumes for a nation in national conflict. An estimated 750,000 Palestinians have been displaced since 1948 and are not fully able to govern, conduct business, or build homes without Israel's permission. Schools closed during the 1987 and 2000 *Intifadat*, and all Palestinians in the Palestinian territories, have dealt with the never-ending hardships of roadblocks, Israeli checkpoints, home raids and home demolishment by Israeli soldiers, lack of water, and frequent power outages.

Statistical improvement does not, however, necessarily result in real-life improvement. *"A scholar who does not produce is like a cloud that does not rain"* is a proverb that Palestinians often reference when describing this disconnect. There is no current research to support this, but a 1996 survey of living conditions in Gaza, the West Bank, and Arab Jerusalem reports:

> Despite the inherent gender bias in curricula, textbooks, goals, facilities, expectations and school ethos, and the segregation of girls in single-sex schools, people cannot acquire an education and remain the same. As the numbers of educated women and girls receiving education have increased, so their perceptions, demands and aspirations are changing. These changes are not proceeding at the same speed in rural areas as in the cities, they do not have the same significance in all social classes, and are not experienced equally by women of different ages, but they have definitely altered the traditional role of women. It is among university women where the changes are deepest: The universities are producing a new generation of educated women, many of whom have a rather different outlook on life, on women's roles, and on political activity than their mothers had. Some of these women now participate in active attempts to bring changes to the lives of other women, especially access to education.[24]

All fifty-five women I interviewed see the positive impact of education in society, and a shift has happened over the years. Every female age eighteen to thirty-five I interviewed has completed anywhere from high school to graduate school. Leila, a twenty-two-year-old law student, believes the priorities of men and women have shifted. "Nowadays women are getting educated and putting marriage on hold," she says. "They're looking to help their future husbands with finances, seeking positions in politics, finance, and upper management. Women now like to learn, teach, and work."

When the participants in this study were asked to rank the importance of education among religion, marriage, and work, receiving an education came a close second to religion. Most of the participants believe it is important to graduate from college before finding a husband or job. Zahra, a twenty-two-year-old college student, echoes what other women in all age groups believe about education.

I wish that every woman could see the importance of education—to see how the world is changing and to see how she can contribute to herself more. By educating herself, she creates awareness for other women in society to want to raise their own value.

Um Basil states:

Back then not only were they [women] not educated, but [they] didn't know how important education could be in a person's life. These same women who were constrained by the times are now saying, "I can give my kids an education even though I was not able to do so for myself." Nowadays women know the strength of education.

If you look at America when I was growing up, women couldn't do a lot of things. Then they changed the laws, and everyone, including women, became free to do whatever they want.

A common stereotype about the Arab region is that women are uneducated. The opposite is true. Except in Yemen, Iraq, and Bahrain, the education levels for women across the Middle East are high. In Kuwait, Qatar, Bahrain, Palestine, United Arab Emirates, Israel, Lebanon, Saudi Arabia, Jordan, and Oman, 50 to 64 percent of college graduates are women.[25]

The education levels of the fifty-five women in this study are as follows:

Twenty-five are enrolled in college or are university graduates.

Three have earned an associate's degree.

Five have earned a master's degree.

Three have completed high school.

Eight completed anywhere from seventh to tenth grade.

Four completed anywhere from first to sixth grade.

Seven received no schooling.

When we break these statistics down by age group, we see that every single female in this study between eighteen and thirty-five years of age has at least finished high school. The idea of zero schooling for females has been eliminated in less than two generations.

As sixty-four-year-old Nour eloquently states, "Education is the key to protecting a woman. If her husband dies, divorces her, or wants to be with another woman, she has the power to take care of herself. If you have an income and retirement plan, it means you have an opinion in the household."

Chapter Four

Labor Market: You Can Have Apricots Tomorrow

We tend to think of third-world women as being oppressed and impoverished, but there's a different narrative that demonstrates highly qualified women in today's emerging markets. However, there is a problem when Middle Eastern societies place such high emphasis on the virtue of a woman but cannot respect and support her decision to enter the workplace. In 2011 the Palestinian Women's Research and Documentation Center (PARC), an institution that promotes women's rights and empowers Palestinian women in the economic, political, and cultural domains found the following:

Unlike the US and other Westernized countries such as the UK and Australia, where women make up to 48% of the workforce, no more than 14% of Palestinian labor market is made up of women. In fact, Palestinian women have the lowest percentage of the work force compared to neighboring countries—36% in Jordan, 38% in Syria, 40% in Lebanon and 46% in Egypt.[26]

Historically, Palestinian women, like many women around the world, took care of the household and worked the fields, but they were not paid for their time. There is little data regarding women's participation in the labor market. It was considered part of women's duties to tend to agricultural needs such as tilling, planting, and harvesting crops to feed their families; their time was not compensated with money. Over time Palestinian women began to go to *souks* (markets) to sell crops to supplement their husbands' incomes.

Another recent study by PARC (2009) observes a gap between the high unemployment rate of Palestinian women and the 2000 Palestinian Labor Law, which states, "Work is the right of every capable citizen" and regulates "the work of women and prohibits discrimination between men and women."[27]

Even though Palestinian females constitute more than half of students enrolled in universities, these enrollment statistics do not translate into an increase in job opportunities or take into account women's full participation in the workforce.

The percentage of unpaid working women increased from 26.9 percent in 2001 to 32.5 percent in 2003 and 33.3 percent in 2005, in comparison with 6.1 percent, 7.1 percent, and 6.3 percent of men for the same years respectively.[28] The Israeli occupation has limited job opportunities for Palestinians; when jobs decrease, women are the first to lose their positions and the last to be rehired because of the belief that men are responsible for providing financial stability to households. Of course this belief does not reflect reality, as many women pay for household expenses and take care of the children.

Another study completed with the support of PARC found several reasons why Palestinian women's roles have not developed. First, as mentioned, Palestinian culture is based on women raising children and believes that finding work outside the home is a man's duty and social value, while women's main duties are limited to the domestic sphere. The statistics reveal that more than one-third of women who work do not earn any monetary compensation, which means they are not bringing in any revenue to promote their self-sufficiency, education, or healthcare. Second, most of the available work is through family-owned enterprises or farms, which are often poorly organized, highly seasonal, and do not contribute to training workers or improving their competency.[29]

Furthermore, the tense political climate and poor economy, coupled with the fact that the Palestinian labor market is closely tied to that of Israel's labor market, affects job opportunities for both males

and females. Finally the jobs available for women
are in occupations for which wages are low and for
which women are paid less than men in those same
positions.[30]

However, there are success stories related to
women and the job market. Samiha Khalil, the
woman who ran against Yasser Arafat for the presi-
dency of the Palestinian territories in 1996, was
best known for her social service institution In'ash
al-Usra, or Society for the Rehabilitation of the
Family. This was an organization founded in 1965
with a budget of $500; by 1986 its budget grew to
$42,000. Founded singlehandedly by Khalil, In'ash
al-Usra ran an orphanage for children of the martyrs,
a nursery school, a bakery, a beautician-training program, a dental clinic, a library, a folklore museum,
and a textile shop. The organization offered literacy
classes and a university scholarship program for
three hundred female students, and employed 4,800
women, working from their own homes, as produc-
ers of traditional Palestinian embroidery. The society
also employed 152 full-time employees, registered
two hundred women in its various vocational training programs, offered a financial sponsorship program for 1,500 families, and ran a program to assist
political prisoners and their families.

Based in al-Bireh (near Ramallah), the organization dedicated itself to helping women and families
by offering self-help programs, as opposed to promoting institutional reform. Much of its budget
came from marketing its own products. When the

first *Intifadah* broke out, Khalil devoted her efforts to assisting its victims and their families.

Um Khalil also published a journal called *Society and Heritage*, which was first issued in 1973 under the direction of a special committee of In'ash al-Usra. The seasonal journal is still being published; it concentrates on folklore and society in general and is run by a group of professionals.

Um Khalil was not one to accept charity or donations that did not meet her patriotic standards. When the Israelis closed her organization in an effort to calm the atmosphere during the *Intifadah,* her defenders claimed that the organization was engaged in social, rather than political, activities. She, herself, however, continued to assert the political nature of her activities. She explained at one time that "teaching women self-reliance is political; making products that compete with Israeli goods, even on a small scale, is political. Self-help is political. It means that we are people seeking and deserving self-determination instead of occupation."[31]

The Palestinian economy is considered to be an emerging market, but with only 14 percent participation in the labor market, it ranks much lower than the bloc of emerging markets called BRIC (Brazil, Russia, India, China). This group of countries makes up 40 percent of the world's population and accounts for 45 percent of global growth since 2007, compared to 20 percent from G-7 economies.[32] In these societies women are outperforming men in higher education—60 percent of Brazilian college graduates and

65 percent of Chinese college graduates are women. We also find they are outperforming US women in the workplace. Brazilian women are being hired for senior management positions in far greater numbers than women are in the United States. In 2009 women held about 40 percent of all jobs in Brazil, leading South America in its share of female workers in the labor force. In addition Brazilian women held 45 percent of managerial jobs and 30 percent of executive positions, compared to 20 percent in the United States. Approximately 11 percent of companies in Brazil have female CEOs, according to the World Economic Forum's *2010 Corporate Gender Gap Report*, making Brazil one of the top five of the thirty-four countries surveyed, after Finland, Norway, and Turkey. In 2011 *Forbes* published an article titled "Winning the War for Talent in Emerging Markets: Why Women Are the Solution," which states the following about Russian women and work.

> The Soviet Union, for all its flaws, indoctrinated the country with the idea that women should work. For the 70 years of the Soviet system's existence, "it was considered bourgeois for a woman not to work," as one management consultant who grew up under Communism recalls. Similarly, under Communism, girls were given the same educational opportunities as boys, and the precedent continues—although women take greater advantage of those opportunities: 86 percent of Russian women aged 18–23 were enrolled in tertiary education, as opposed

to only 64 percent of the men. They want to use their degrees to do something more than quote Pushkin. As a female senior executive at a Russian- based company told us, "A woman wants to have a career because otherwise she wouldn't be interesting."[33]

The key point here is that Palestinian society has not fully viewed Palestinian women as an asset in the workplace. Furthermore, as Palestinian females are exceeding the number of Palestinian men enrolled in college, there is now a great opportunity for Palestinian women to position themselves in the global market—as long as there is a solution to allow Palestinians to freely govern themselves without Israeli control.

One of the major constraints on growing the Palestinian market is the separation barrier Israel started to build in 2002. The following excerpt from a United Nations Trade and Development Conference states in detail the economic hardships imposed on Palestinians by the wall.

While the barrier revealed adverse effects on Palestinian socio-economic conditions, its full impact has yet to be realized. The barrier encircles the northern West Bank cities and surrounding areas of Jenin, Qalqilya and Tulkarem, the central cities of Ramallah, northern Bethlehem, Jerusalem and their vicinity and the southern areas covering cities such as Bethlehem, Hebron and areas around them, creating an enclosed-zone of Palestine territory between the United Nations Armistice line (the Green Line) and the barrier. These areas cover some 142,640 acres, representing around 10 percent of the area of the West Bank (including Jerusalem). These areas will be enveloped with a system of fences, ditches, razor wire, groomed trace sands, electronic monitoring systems and patrol roads which people and goods are authorized to pass through certain gates during limited, irregular hours.

According to the most recent published maps, when completed, the barrier will be 670 km long, of which only 20 percent will run along the Green Line. Its effective length will be twice that of the Green Line (315 km), since 85 percent of the barrier intrudes in the West Bank to a depth of 22 kilometers in some areas. The cities of Qalqilya, Bethlehem, Tulkarem and Jerusalem will be surrounded or divided by 8-meter high concrete slab segments connected to form a wall.

Around 50,000 Palestinians living in 38 villages and towns will be confined to areas situated between the Green Line and the barrier, of which some 5,000 will live in "closed areas" or "enclaves," totally surrounded by the barrier. The rest will either live in "semi- enclaves," surrounded by the barrier and connected with the rest of the West Bank by only one route, and "closed areas," between the barrier and the Green Line. Palestinians living outside these enclaves and closed areas as well as those living outside the wall should apply for permits to reach their jobs and farms, while those living in closed areas should obtain special permits to maintain their residency rights. These permits are valid for up to six months and can only be used to cross a single designated gate.

The barrier's construction has also led to the confiscation of around 27,055 hectares (270 sq. km) of land by February 2004, including some of the most fertile areas in the West Bank (WB), as well as 49 wells. In addition to this the destruction of physical infrastructures, leaving 22 percent of the West Bank areas surrounding the barrier without road and water networks, and nearly 50 percent of the residents without access to health services. Actually, the barrier is effectively setting the limits to the development prospects of the West Bank, isolating enterprises from their main export and local markets and increasing the risks associated with new investments. The construction works have forced 952 enterprises to shut down by the end of March 2004.

The area of land under the PA's full civil jurisdiction in the West Bank is limited to only 3 percent. At the same time, the Palestinian economy remains subject to Israeli control measures.[34]

The Palestinian social reality has produced two issues that relate to women's participation in the labor market. The first issue is determining the scope of jobs or occupations for which women can compete. The second is the fact that even though public policy had women's empowerment on its social agenda for years, it was never transformed into actual programs, and change in this area is still low. Entering the labor market demonstrates a need rather than a developmental option or perhaps the last option a woman may resort to for improving her social and economic situation.[35]

Ultimately every challenge needs a solution. The Palestinian-Israeli conflict needs a great deal of love, patience, and compassion in order to not only solve the economic constraints, but also heal emotional, physical, and spiritual traumas both sides have endured. When humanity can dissolve internal barriers, the physical walls that separate people crumble. Only when we see ourselves as brothers, sisters, lovers, and caretakers, and consciously bring light and awareness into our situations, can the problems of our world, including the Palestinian-Israeli conflict, be resolved. When we put away our guns and extend our hands to our neighbors, only then can we see one another as one—one people looking to grow, thrive, and feel joy in everyday life.

The Economic Value of a Housewife

What is the economic value of a housewife? Historically the economic value of a Palestinian woman has been tied to her services as a mother, wife, and caretaker of all things related to the household—with the exception of financial decisions. If only housewives were bought and sold in an open market like wheat futures, we could have an accurate measure of their worth. To paraphrase Oscar Wilde, economists often know the price of everything but the value of nothing. Economists have argued for two different methods to measure the value of a housewife—the opportunity cost method and the replacement cost method.[36]

With regard to calculating the value of a housewife, the fundamental idea behind the opportunity cost (OC) method is "What does the household sacrifice by having the wife stay at home to work?" In other words what is the *opportunity cost* of the housewife's time? If a female lawyer earns $150 an hour, and she decides to forgo an hour of work to do the dishes, the cost of that task is $150. Economists then say that the $150 measures the value of an hour of housewife service.

According to Allen's 2010 published research in the American Journal of Family Law, the replacement cost (RC) approach to the problem asks, "How much would it cost to replace the services of the housewife?" The idea is that one could go into the marketplace; find the wage for nannies, cooks, et cetera; then use these wages to calculate the value of housewife services. Sometimes an average is used; sometimes the wage within each specialty is used.

Both of these methods are riddled with well-known problems:

They measure the value of household services *at the margin and not the total value.*

The OC approach assumes a woman's hours of work are completely flexible.

The RC approach assumes the productivity of the wife and market replacement are the same.

Both methods have difficulty dealing with full-time, long-term housewives who have been separated from the labor market for years.

Both methods rely on often-arbitrary measures of time devoted to household services.

Both methods are silent regarding how to treat housewife services that are not available in the market.

Both methods have difficulty dealing with the commingling of leisure and household services.

Allen also states that the fundamental problem with both methods is that they are based on market-oriented economic theory, and as a result, they ignore the *institutional* aspect of marriage. Marriage, as an institution, is designed to produce a set of goods that *the market does not produce.* Certainly some market goods are jointly produced in the marriage, but these are secondary to the main purpose of marriage. Marriage restricts the behavior of both the husband and wife such that they have an incentive over their lifecycle to cooperate in procreation and the successful rearing of the next generation. To confuse the value of a housewife with the services of a domestic servant misses the point entirely. Market-based procedures are crude, unreliable, and biased, and underestimate the true value of a housewife.

Within the past twenty-five years, economists have started to move away from this purely market-based way of thinking and have begun to consider the institutional aspects of exchange. This work leads to an interesting method of evaluating the worth of a housewife—one that works best in cases in which here the market approach works poorly.

Marriage is a sharing arrangement. A husband does not hire his wife, nor does the wife hire her husband. When the marriage is doing well, both benefit, and in hard times, both suffer. As the saying goes, they marry "for better or for worse." Some shares are better than others. A spouse who gets a small share of the pie has little incentive to work within the marriage. The gains from an increased share to this person will more than offset the disincentives caused by reducing the share to the other spouse. Economists have shown there is an "optimal share" that creates the best incentives for the husband and wife to contribute to the marriage.

This does not mean the type of contributions are the same. The husband may be expected to work in the labor force while the wife may work in the home full time. Nor does it mean the contributions actually end up being equal. It simply means the couple believes at the time of marriage that the two different streams of services are of equal value; otherwise they wouldn't marry. Thus this approach recognizes the most valuable contribution of a full-time housewife—giving birth and raising children. The other methods, which focus on simple household chores, ignore the most important contributions of the wife.

Recognizing the incentives of sharing within a marriage explains why marriages have a difficult time surviving large unexpected shocks such as infertility or long spells of unemployment. An option to divorce is to renegotiate the share. However, renegotiation, *ex post,* always will imply a suboptimal share. The spouse who ends up, *ex post,* more productive always will be better off finding a new mate of similar productivity.[37]

However, not all societies believe in the value of a housewife. For example, in her July 2010 *New York Times* article "The Stigma of Being a Housewife," Katrin Bennhold points out:

> When the Swedish journalist Peter Letmark tried to track down a housewife for a series on 21st-century parents in the newspaper *Dagens Nyheter* recently, he failed. Letmark explained, "Housewives are a near extinct species in Sweden. And the few who still do exist don't really dare to go public with it....

> In the 1950s, women were expected to stay at home, and those who wanted to work were often stigmatized. Today it's mostly the other way round, pitting women against one another along the fault lines of conviction, economic class and need, and, often, ethnicity.

> Across the developed world, women who stay home are increasingly seen as old-fashioned and an economic burden to society. If their husbands are rich, they are frequently berated for being

lazy; if they are immigrants, for keeping children from learning the language and ways of their host country.

Their daily chores of cleaning, cooking or raising their children have always been ignored by national accounts. (If a man marries his housekeeper and stops paying her for her work, G.D.P. goes down. If a woman stops nursing and buys formula for her baby, G.D.P. goes up.) In a debate that counts women catching up with men in education and the labor market in terms of raising productivity and economic growth, stay-at-home moms are valued less than ever. This is so despite the fact that from Norway to the United States, economists put the value of their unpaid work ahead of that of the manufacturing sector.

In countries where mothers still struggle to combine career with family and quit work less out of conviction than out of necessity, they are often doubly punished. In Germany, the biggest economy in Europe, most schools still finish at lunchtime, and full-time nurseries for children under 3 are scarce. Yet in this generation of young mothers you are more likely to find women saying they are on extended maternity leave or between jobs than admitting they are housewives.

Only among the wealthy is it seen as class status when the highly educated mother takes children to Chinese or violin lessons.[38]

Does it come down to pay or value? Working and nonworking mothers still do most of the unpaid work in their homes—even in Sweden.

In essence a Palestinian woman's role in the household is not appreciated for its full value. Her contributions as a cook, cleaner, grocery shopper, and personal assistant (i.e., running errands and dropping her kids off at activities) all adds up to time that is taken away from herself. In addition to acknowledging the often underappreciated roles of women, we should note that all of our lives revolve around a business-related activity. Palestinian women may not be paid for what they do at home, but their duties are part of their social capital that helps support the Palestinian society in its role as a powerful social structure. Without women's help in this area, what kind of society would Palestinians have? More and more Palestinian women are now looking to be compensated for their work as professionals as opposed to working in family business settings.

Chapter Five

Religion—From God We Come and to God We Return

Asking a practicing Palestinian Muslim or Christian whether religion is important is like asking whether two eyes are better than one. "It's how we're born," says thirty-five year old researcher Nadia.

Reema, a college educated sixty-two-year-old mother of four, gives her interpretation.

> People don't understand religion. I practice Islam, which is very similar to Christianity. Religion taught us how to greet each other, respect each other, treat each other in marriage, et cetera, and the reason why Americans and the United States hold on to the things that aren't true in Islam is because they can't find someone following it properly to correctly explain it to them. If we [the

> Palestinians] aren't living it right in our country, how
> do we expect Americans to respect us? They see that our
> customs are wrong and believe our religion is wrong,
> when it is the way we [Palestinians] treat each other as
> wrong, not the religion itself.

> If you want someone to respect your religion, then you
> [need to] respect the religion.

Thirty-seven of the Palestinian women I interviewed believe that religion is **very important,** and nine believe it is **important.** "Religion is the compass to everything," emphasizes forty-one-year-old Lina.

Not all Palestinians in this study agree. Nine out of the fifty-five women do not believe a person needs to be religious to have faith, including Samira. She is a slender nineteen-year-old woman with dark eyes and long black hair. She grew up covering her hair with a *mandeela* but decided to uncover her hair after she got married. Her husband has no opinion on the subject and loves her for who she is. Samira, like many young women, feels more comfortable wearing Western-style clothes: jeans, T-shirts, and sneakers. She does not believe religion is the most important thing in life. Samira further explains:

> It's not about duty; it's what calls you from within.
> Prayer can be a very personal thing without showing
> that you're doing it in front of the world. But some
> people are afraid and publicly enforce hijab. If you are
> a good Muslim that believes in God, then there is no
> reason to fear people.

Twenty-two-year-old Rula agrees with Samira. She says, "Religion isn't that important because it's part of your value system. You don't have to be religious to have faith."

According to other Palestinian women, religion is the source of conflict and bloodshed, not enlightenment. Rania, a seventy-nine-year-old woman who was very involved with the women's social movement in the late 1960s says:

I am a Christian, and my grandfather was a Christian pastor. We went to church, but we didn't believe in all the appearances of church—we didn't embellish with crosses, et cetera, at that time. We had Muslims come with us to church. All I remember is that we were Arab. Muslims and Christians were one; it was an Arab and Palestinian awakening. As Palestine became more threatened, the religious element became much more strong.

That was the generation I grew up in. It used to be that only a few people attended a holy sanctuary, but now everyone goes to church or mosque. I am spiritual by nature and believe in values, but after 1967 I stopped going to church. I believe the teachings are the same in all these religions. But most people are born into religion, and it becomes deeply entrenched within them. It takes a lot to be liberated from it.

Every religion is saying the same thing—give to the poor and love your neighbor. But yet we're fighting in the name of religion.

Samar agrees with Rania. She is a fifty-three-year-old mother of three who earned a master's degree in her thirties. A director of a major research center, she states:

> Religion has never been part of my life. I'm a socialist and a secularist. I really put my work and family at the same level and was able to do them both by finding the right formula for myself. I have a husband who supports me fully, and we shared all the roles and duties. I believe that's why we have very good children who are performing very well academically and socially.

The early 1900s was a time when God was everywhere, but there was no ideal way of living as a Muslim, Jew, or Christian. Religion was less institutionalized and more spiritual during this period. People emphasized doing the right thing as well as the importance of getting along with their neighbors.[39] Life offered a thousand blessings, but people were cautious about extending their hands to those who were greedy or dishonest.[40] Women covered their hair not in the name of religion but to distinguish between the wealthy and lower economic classes. Palestinian women born into wealthy families covered their hair as a fashion statement and out of modesty, not because of religion.

Before the late 1940s, most Muslims did not observe demanding religious practices and paid attention only to those traditional Islamic teachings that had been fully incorporated into the culture as a part of everyday behavior. Very few people paid *zakat* (tithing) faithfully. Very few fasted during the month of Ramadan. In the village of Beitin, only 5 percent fasted the entire month. Only rarely did more than two dozen people in Beitin pray regularly during this period. As far as making a pilgrimage to Mecca was concerned, only two Beitin couples ever have made the journey in the past half-century—and they might have made the trip for reasons that were not entirely religious.[41]

What changed?

The 1948 *Nakba* marked the first major event that changed society's perceptions of religion.[42] It was a year when more than 750,000 Palestinians fled or were forced to leave their homes, and the state of Israel was born. Palestinians began to feel more threatened and aware of God as a source of protection and guidance through life's tribulations. Palestinian women and men visibly became more conservative. The division between the secular and sacred became blurred. Palestinian Christians and Muslims turned to religion as their social and political compass. Women, who historically only wore the *mandeela* (head scarf) as a cultural statement, now began to wear it as a religious statement.

The 1967 Arab-Israeli War and two Palestinian uprisings against the Israeli occupation (in 1988 and 2000) further advanced religious conservatism among Muslims, Christians, and Jews. However, after the attacks on US soil on September 11, 2001, the entire Middle East began a trend toward conservatism. More Palestinians began to pray in mosques and churches. Muslims felt "their" Islam was being put on trial and that they had to prove their innocence.

In 2007 *Anthropology Today* published an interview with Akbar Ahmed, who holds the Ibn Khaldun Chair of Islamic Studies at American University in Washington, DC. Akbar explains why there is a rise in Islam conservatism in Gustaaf Houtman's report:

> Overnight we saw people who were clueless about society, culture and religion giving lectures on precisely those subjects in Islam. Those who called themselves "security experts" and "terrorism analysts" were everywhere. Much of what they had to say was little more than concoction of prejudice, ignorance and sometimes plain stupidity. The result was that a great opportunity for an effective contribution of anthropology to world affairs was missed. Much of the growing antagonism between the West and the Muslim world could have been minimized or even avoided if anthropologists had been heard in the earlier days.

> 9/11 transformed the world and those Muslims who want violence are partly to blame. The rest of the blame falls squarely on the shoulders of those who are not Muslim and who could have responded with a different strategy. Instead of alienating the vast body of the Muslim world they could have reached out through dialogue and understanding and thereby marginalized the

extremists. By failing to do so they only swelled the ranks of those Muslims who believe that they are standing up to defend their faith, which they see as being under attack.[43]

There are misconceptions regarding Islam's teachings and its role in women's lives. Muslims believe Islam is a complete system that offers answers to any questions a person has in his or her life. This includes rights to property, the treatment of all individuals, birth and burial customs, what to eat, whom to marry, and how to settle disputes. Muslims believe that God does not judge people based on their gender or race but on what is in their hearts. Islam gives a woman the right to inherit property, choose a spouse, and divorce. Islam also instructs societies to educate both men and women. Culturally, however, some Arab-region countries choose to implement rules that contradict the teachings of Islam.

Chapter Six

Dress Code: Fashion or Faith?

While honor, modesty, and family are the social fabrics woven together in Palestinian society's belief system, the rules regarding the acceptable ways to function and to portray these values differ within each family. For example if a woman from a poor village family marries into a wealthy family from the city, she is more likely to come and go as she pleases, day or night, and set her daily schedule of activities. She is more likely to dress differently than she did in the village and not worry about people gossiping about her, as they would in the village. However, when visiting family in the village, she is more likely to follow the behavior and social rules with which she grew up—dressing and behaving in accordance with the community's customs.

Many people may perceive this as living a double life, or passing as "a way for us to be seen or unseen," writes Dr. Marcia Alesan Dawkins, author of the 2012 book *Clearly Invisible: Racial Passing and the Color of Cultural Identity.* Dawkins explains:

> Passing shifts our social positions amidst social limitations…but if we pay attention, passing can reveal our collective blind spots as well as our individual similarities and differences. Passing forces us to think and rethink what exactly makes a person black, white, or "other," and why we care. It helps us create worlds we can actually live in. And it makes us think about the ties and binds of pleasure, language, and action. It makes us consider the hazards of silence and the hope of communication. (p. xi)

In her book Dawkins describes six methods of passing: persuasion, property, power, principle, pastime, and paradox. Passing via power involves "cultural practices of resistance and is also rhetorical. Rhetorical power is the capacity of discourse to direct or influence behavior inside and outside of traditional discursive constraints."[44] In this context a Palestinian woman from a village who marries into a wealthy family from the city passes in two ways in order to fit into two lifestyles: 1) to maximize the benefits of honoring and pleasing her parents; and 2) to move into a social class that allows greater autonomy and freedom.

This brings us to an interesting question about the *hijab*, the Islamic dress code whereby a woman wears loosely fitted clothing and a headscarf. Is this a form of oppression—as seen by many Westerners as a conservative religious practice—a cultural trend, or a way to navigate through society with greater autonomy or freedom? While some Middle Eastern countries such as Saudi Arabia and Yemen enforce the wearing of the *hijab* on all females, other governments—such as Jordan, Lebanon, Palestine, and Turkey—do not. The Quran directs both men and women to dress modestly, but the actual interpretation and implementation of this rule varies enormously. Hair is considered part of a woman's physical attractiveness, which is why it is often covered. Traveling to the Holy Land, one can observe Jewish and Palestinian Christian women who also cover their hair for the sake of modesty. Also the *hijab* is only one aspect of Muslim practice; it is often wrongly emphasized over more important aspects because of its visibility. Many Muslim women choose not to wear a *hijab* or believe wearing it is not necessary to be a virtuous Muslim.

There is also confusion surrounding the full-body veil, or *burqa*, which is an accessory, not the system of Islamic dress code known as the *hijab*. Like the headscarf, the veil historically has been related to social class, not religion. The veil was first adopted from pre-Islamic Byzantine and Persian customs. In most areas, poor and rural women have covered themselves less often than urban and elite women. Within Islam head coverings vary by culture. They range from loose scarves to veils and full-length coverings, such as the *burqa* worn by many Afghan women. Covering the face was more common in the past than it is today and is practiced more often in some regions than others. Head coverings are not solely a facet of Islam, however, and women of many cultures and religions cover their heads in different ways.[45]

Veiling rules vary from country to country. In the modern period, strict laws about women's dress are often used to emphasize the religious orientation of a particular government, as in Iran or Saudi Arabia. On the other hand, Turkey does not allow women to wear veils in public offices or universities because the Turkish state is committed to a more secular identity.

There's also the misconception that, if given the choice, Arab and Muslim women would choose not to wear *hijab*. This study cannot give voice to all of the Arab or Muslim women in the world regarding how they feel about the *hijab* or *burqa*. The *burqa* and *niqab* (head covering), however, are not commonly worn in Palestinian culture.

It wasn't until a conversation with two female friends at lunch one day that I realized Westerners generally do not understand the dress code in the Arab region. One friend is in her thirties and the other in her eighties, and both are highly intellectual. I said something along the lines of, "The *burqa* and *niqab* aren't part of the Palestinian dress code. It's unusual to see women dressed this way. They're probably from somewhere else in the Middle East."

Both ladies offered blank stares and replied, "Really?" In this moment I acknowledged my ignorance and my innocent assumption that people are aware of the fact that not all Arabs in the Middle East dress the same, nor do all Arab societies adopt the various forms of women's coverings.

Some Palestinian women, however, are forced to wear the *hijab*, either by their parents or societal pressures. Twenty-two-year-old Iman says, "There are some villages that force their women to wear *hijab*. Even though there is no law that says so, it's a custom that's been adopted by a conservative society."

Other women wear the *hijab* by choice, such as twenty-two-year-old Amani. She says, "I started to get into religion in the tenth grade. That's when I decided to wear the *jilbab* and cover my hair. I stopped wearing revealing outfits."

Over my years of traveling to Palestinian villages and cities, I realized that one is more likely to see a woman from the village cover her hair than one from a city such as Ramallah or Nablus. One day a woman may wear a *jilbab*, the next day jeans and a long shirt, and another day a stylish dress that, again, still covers her body. Some wear makeup and show their earrings, but you won't see their hair. In other words, some women still care about style, even if their hair is covered and they are dressed modestly. The Arabic word for these women is *muhajjabat*. In the United States we jokingly call these women *muhajja*-babes!

For the purpose of this study, I asked Palestinian women how they dress and whether this has changed since they were young. In other words does their dress code differ from that of their mothers, grand-mothers, or daughters?

Nineteen-year-old newlywed Samira acknowl-edges that the dress code has changed over the years. She says:

> I know my mom is a traditional woman who covers her hair and dresses modestly, but I'm into Western style clothes—jeans, T-shirts, and tennis shoes. In the old days, people had to wear what they had. They were lucky to have more than three outfits. Now people dress fashionably and follow international trends.

Twenty-five-year-old Shadia explains the trend of wearing the traditional Palestinian costume, or *thoub*.

> Women like my grandmother always wore a thoub, regardless of what time of the day. They wore them every day and at weddings. Nowadays we just wear thwaab at ceremonies and dress normal the rest of the time (in pants, skirts, and tops). I never wear a thoub, except when I want to take special pictures.

I grew up around Palestinian culture, and it's always been hard for me to decipher the dress code—why some women choose to wear the *thoub* all the time while others wear it exclusively at weddings. There are no exact reasons why over time some women become more or less conservative, tradi-tional, or fashionable in the way they dress. From what I gather, many factors influence their decisions:

personal choice, societal pressures, change in economic status or family structure, shift in cultural norms, social class, fashion trends, and preservation of heritage. It is similar to what I've observed growing up in the United States—there is no simple explanation as to why women dress the way they do.

A few women acknowledge that their parents force them to wear the *hijab*. However, they are quick to clarify that the *hijab* is not pushed on them for purely religious reasons. The reasons vary based on upbringing (class, status, and education level) and are a simple reflection on the parents' ideals. Furthermore, clothing restrictions placed on Palestinian girls are no different than the types of clothing restrictions American parents often enforce on their teenage daughters. Twenty-seven-year-old Hala is one semester shy of earning her master's degree. She admits that she has voluntarily worn the *jilbab* since she was a teenager, but as an adult she challenges this decision. Hala says:

> *I've been wearing jilbab since I was fourteen. I did it on my own. But how can any fourteen-year-old know anything about religion? I feel like my parents should have questioned my decision. If my daughter at fourteen came to me said, "I want to wear the jilbab," I wouldn't let her, because she is not of age to make these kinds of decisions. I'm not ultra religious or anything, but I can only teach her what Islam says or doesn't say, and it's up to her how religious she wants to be when she's older.*

This begs us to ask, "What is the appropriate age to understand God and religion?"

Some Palestinian women continue to wear the *hijab* when they are older, while others abandon it. Religious and nonreligious women, strong and weak women, and all kinds of women in between, wear the *hijab*, which also can be said of the veil. It may be worn by choice or obligation. Some women wear the *hijab* occasionally, while others wear it exclusively in public.

Chapter Seven

Thoub: Preserving Heritage

This brings us to an interesting point in the discussion—the *thoub*, or traditional Palestinian dress. Author Widad Kawar is one of the few people in Palestinian society who has documented the cultural meaning of the traditional Palestinian costume called the *thoub* ("*thwaab*" is the plural form). Kawar grew up in Bethlehem in the 1940s and remembers seeing women from all over the region wearing a *thoub*. Eighty-five-year-old Um Omar says:

> *Palestinian woman have changed the way they dress, but ladies my age haven't changed the way we dress. Girls now wear pants, T-shirts, and dresses, but we've always worn these thwaab.*

Um Omar goes went far as to show me her closet full of colorful *thwaab*. Hand-stitched, a thoub can cost a few hundred to thousands of dollars. One *thoub* can last a lifetime if it is maintained properly.

The *thoub* was and still is more than a fashion statement; it is a symbol of heritage and of belonging. Women in each village incorporate different designs on their *thwaab,* which allows for identification as a Palestinian. At some points the *thoub* also has symbolized the change from being a young girl to becoming a woman. Females who were adults in the 1940s were accustomed to solely wearing a *thoub* since childhood. Young girls in the 1940s and 1950s were accustomed to wearing skirts and blouses until their womanhood years and then switched to wearing *thwaab* as adults. Females growing up in the 1960s made different fashion choices. They included pants in their wardrobe and showed more patriotism in their actions than through the clothes they wore. Now we find *thwaab* in young women's closets, but usually they wear them only to a wedding or *henna* (pre-wedding ceremony). All women, regardless of age, wear the *thoub* to honor their tradition from years past.

In her 1980 book, *The Traditional Palestinian Costume,* Kawar cites historical events that date back to 640 AD as being the main influences on the design and technique of Palestinian embroidery but also notes that they have Byzantine, Greek, Crusade, Ottoman Turkish, Syrian, French, German, Balkan, and Scandinavian influences. She writes:

Each village in Palestine has its own general pattern, and style, or cut of the costume, and its particular unit of specific patterns that has been handed down by memory from mother to daughter. At the same time, one can also notice some outside influences from other areas infiltrating the traditional patterns, for this is an inevitable outcome of intermarriage, visiting, or travel from one location to another.

A village woman reads her patterns like a story. She is proud of them and the perfection of their execution on her costume. For her, the costume is her "passport," a bearer of her identity. On market day, she goes to the big towns, and it is her costume that speaks for her, saying where she comes from, and reflecting her standard of perfection in embroidery, her sense of colour combination and harmony of designs. Now and then, a woman would copy a pattern, which took her fancy, which she might have seen on a visitor's costume or during a trip to the market, but the new combinations soon became typical of one village only; in fact, no two villages in Palestine have the same combination of patterns. To the village woman, this is a matter of village pride and a tradition worth keeping.

The Bethlehem dress, or the *thoub malak*, a special bridal gown made of velvet and embroidered with gold, is one style of dress that spread in many villages of Palestine. Its elegant, rich appearance gave it great distinction. We can find it in the Hebron area, Ramallah and the surrounding villages, and in Majdal near Jaffa. These are general observations on the styles or cut of the Palestinian costumes, yet more can be done to study other peculiarities, for each village has its own distinctiveness in this aspect of Palestinian costume.[46]

Although ethnic and international fashion styles of clothing have come and gone in Palestinian society, the traditional Palestinian dress remains part of the cultural scene.

Chapter Eight

National Activism: One without Land Is One without Honor

The most commonly known side of Palestinians in the West is their fighting side—that is, their participation in the conflict with Israel. News reports recently have shed light on the latest phenomenon of female suicide bombers, as if females instantly have shed their lives at home in exchange for violence.[47] Little is reported on Palestinian women's long-term passion for national liberation and their stance at the forefront of activism. Only a handful of influential Palestinian women in the Palestinian territories have been recognized for their national activism, and they are the same women who have fought for women's rights in society. These women are considered feminists, and perhaps politics has served as the doorway into addressing social issues, which has empowered women to do more than remain housewives when they returned to their homes.

Palestinian women's activism can be traced back to at least 1921, with the founding of the Palestinian Women's Union, which led demonstrations against the Balfour Declaration and organized the General Palestinian Women's Congress in Jerusalem in 1929. Palestinian women have played active roles as well during every stage of their people's struggle. During the 1936–'39 Revolt, Palestinian women cared for the injured, demonstrated, signed petitions, hid rebels, and took up arms to defend their land. In the 1947–'48 war, which resulted in the establishment of the State of Israel, Palestinian women immediately had to assume the responsibility of their families and their nation, thus radically altering their social roles. Between 1948 and 1967, Palestinian women joined various political movements, such as Al-Fatah, founded in 1965 by Yasser Arafat and his colleagues.[48]

The founding of the Palestine Liberation Organization (PLO) in 1964 ushered in a new era of women's activism. The original Palestine Women's Union "participated in the founding meeting of the Palestinian National Council in East Jerusalem in 1964, and branches of the union were formed throughout the West Bank."[49] Operating under the cover of charitable organizations, they organized literacy, sewing, first aid, and nursing courses and founded orphanages, hospitals, and schools. Some Palestinian women in the West Bank also began to participate in nationalist demonstrations and to distribute leaflets, particularly after the onset of the Israeli occupation in 1967.

There were no dramatic shifts in consciousness regarding gender issues among women in the occupied Palestinian territories until well into the 1970s, but a new and different dynamism marked the experiences of women during the Diaspora of 1948. Approximately 750,000 Palestinians were displaced or became refugees.

What does it mean to be a refugee or to become displaced? According to the United Nations High Commissioner for Refugees (UNHCR), the term "refugee" applies to any person who "owning to well-founded fear of being persecuted for reasons of race, religion, nationality, membership of a particular social group or political opinion, is outside the country of his nationality and is unable or, owing to such fear, is unwilling to avail himself to the protection of that country."

According to a refugee woman who was an activist in the 1936–'39 revolt, "The Palestinian used to be much more advanced in his own country, and women were more independent and freer...but after 1948 this changed. In the camps the Palestinian became ultra-strict, even fanatic about the 'honor' of his women. Perhaps this was because he had lost everything that gave his life meaning and 'honor' was the only possession remaining to him."[50] This testimonial, and others like it, was the result of field research conducted by Rosemary Sayigh, British journalist and author of the book, *Palestinians: From Peasants to Revolutionaries.*

Palestinian women fought alongside Palestinian men during the first *Intifadah*, or uprising, against Israeli occupation in 1987 and again in 2000, when the second *Intifadah* ignited. Women and girls played active roles in the struggle, and despite the limitations of their roles in the domestic sphere, "they [Palestinian women] did not sit back and ask the men to grant them freedom and equality; women in the *Intifadah* went out and actually did things. They confronted the army. They built barricades. They threw stones. They helped prevent the arrest of men. They took on-the-spot decisions. Through such actions, and mainly through the creation and management of women's organizations and committees to deal with their problems and needs, they gave up their traditional roles."[51]

Women's movements are linked to the activities of international institutions, mainly nongovernmental organizations, which were working in Palestine on projects aimed at improving women's living conditions and rights. These movements and activities reach every aspect of Palestinian women's lives, and alongside education, they play a role of paramount importance in their liberation process. The influence of women's activities already has been noticed in Palestinian society, but social resistance to change and opposition from men in general, and religious groups in particular, is strong.

Women, Society and Education in Palestine, a study published in 1996 by Agustin Velloso, reveals:

> It is difficult for a man to challenge a woman and say, "No, you can't do this," because she's already done it. The whole system of taboos, and the definitions of honor and shame have changed.... Male responses are complex because, on the one hand, men may welcome greater female participation and even encourage it; at the same time, they cannot help but retain a residual, and often not even fully articulated, determination to preserve traditional male privileges. It could be said that men are scared and uncomfortable with women's new roles, which is not unique to Palestine. Religious groups feel themselves under more direct attack since women's initiatives strike at their foundations.[52]

According to one interviewee who was part of the national movement to liberate Palestine in the 1960s, Hamas was founded to help the social needs of Palestinians and also to promote their political agenda. They introduced many programs—not only political activities, but also educational activities, sanitation projects, sports programs, and social projects. In terms of cultural activities, Hamas has been active in maintaining sports programs. Like secular reform groups, Hamas also has participated in many workshops, conferences, and conventions in calling for the peace process.

However, the secular social groups could not provide service and advice, or provide funds as quickly or on as large a scale as Hamas could. And during times of need, the needy turned to God. Hamas embodied religion and a political agenda and was popular because the Palestinian people were tired of Fatah's inability to fulfill their promises of helping Palestinians find peace. Hamas gained popularity through its social service campaigns, which was a way to build support for its political agendas. Hamas, which appealed to the villagers, also had deeper pockets than nongovernment organizations (NGOs), which were mainly established in the cities. NGO employees needed more time to connect with villagers. Although NGOs were effective in changing lives, they were not able to do it as quickly or on as large a scale as Hamas.

Overall NGOs struck at Hamas's foundation because social movements were giving voice to women's issues and empowering women through education and work. Hamas wasn't concerned with women's rights, just their votes.

It is also important to highlight the role of Palestinian women's volunteer organizations and grassroots committees in the struggle for national and women's rights. NGOs are mainly research centers that provide important studies and data to support the activities of the women's movement, which was originally spearheaded by the General Union of

Palestinian Women (GUPW), and includes all women's volunteer societies and grassroots committees.

From the mid 1960s to mid 1980s, one influential woman in particular was very good at connecting with various members of villages. She knew that excluding men and religious leaders wasn't the way to gain support for women's empowerment. Instead of declaring her opposition to the concept of the *hamula* (the social kinship structure of a large extended family), Samiha Khalil found a way around it. She spoke to the village *imam* and elder men and women in communities to gain their support. Khalil secured their respect and trust, which allowed her message to be well received by the rest of the community.

In 2013 women are actively fighting in the forefront alongside Palestinian men by co-facilitating demonstrations in villages close to the Green Line, mainly in Ni'lin and Bi'lin.

Palestinian women always have been involved in the political lives of their people. "Women's active participation, however, was not sufficient to radically alter the status quo in gender relations. This was due to the Palestinian movement's view that national liberation was its first and only priority."[53]

I didn't directly ask my interviewees about the Israeli occupation, but when asked, "What are the biggest challenges facing Palestinian women your age?" seven women included the phrase "national liberation" as part of their answers.

Despite the weight of tradition and the pressure exerted by religious and traditionalist groups that are working against women's equality in education and social fields, a trend in favor of women's rights also can be detected in contemporary Palestinian society. Both opposing currents, each with its own supporting ideas and facts, are fighting for supremacy at a time when Palestinian society is fully immersed in the difficult process of re-creating itself and establishing self-rule. Both currents think very differently about the role of Palestinian women in this process. It is far from easy to assess the situation, let alone the future, because, on the one hand, "taking part in the national struggle, however, has not automatically been translated into gains and status," and on the other, "the experience women are gaining in the national struggle is serving them well in raising their consciousness for the need to fight for their rights."[54]

The bottom line is that the Palestinian and Israeli governments can be with the people, or against the people, but they are not stopping Palestinian society, especially women, from being heard.

Chapter Nine

Stories: Palestinian Monologues

Let us now take a look at some individual stories of Palestinian women, from within and outside the study, to fully appreciate their voices and perspectives.

Story #1—Life Is Not about Duty; It's What Calls You from Within

Samira is a beautiful, slender, nineteen-year-old woman with dark eyes and long black hair. She grew up in the Palestinian village of Beitin and recently married a Palestinian-American man. She is awaiting her paperwork so that she can come to the United States and isn't afraid to speak her mind about her culture. She grew up covering her hair with a *mandeela* but decided to uncover her hair after she got married. Her husband has no opinion on the subject and loves her for who she is. Samira, like many young women, is more comfortable wearing Western-style clothes—jeans, T-shirts, and sneakers. She does not believe religion is the most important thing in life. "It's not about duty; it's what calls you from within. Prayer can be a very personal thing without showing that you're doing it in front of the world. But some people are afraid, and they enforce *hijab*. If you are a good Muslim, then there is no reason to fear people." Although Samira is married, she believes having her own identity is very important because she can prove to the world that she can make it through life with or without a man. She aspires to study journalism and become a reporter.

Story #2—Upgrading Traditions

Um Omar is eighty-eight years old and lives in Beitin. Her first and only marriage was to a man who already was married to another woman, but she had a very fulfilling life with him. She was twenty-four years old when she married. She has had no schooling but learned how to write her name for legal purposes. She grew up working mainly in agriculture and around the house: tilling, planting, sewing, cultivating the land, and selling olive oil, figs, and vegetables. When she was growing up, "a woman didn't really have a role in society. Her role was to be a bride who gave birth to children, kept things clean, cooked, raised the kids, et cetera, while her husband worked outside the house." Um Omar also says, "Back then a woman never gave her opinion. She was just told what to do by her husband and in-laws. But women's roles are much better now. They don't have to work the fields day and night to put food on the table. They can also do things on their own." Um Omar says she would like society to relax its rules regarding women so that they do not need to receive permission to do things without the approval of their extended families. Although it's important for a woman to know who she is, Um Omar believes it is equally important to find balance with a husband. "It's not good for her to be completely on her own in life," she says. "It's important for her to have a good personality and find the right man for her."

Story #3—Rising above Limitations

Sarah, a fifty-three-year-old single woman in Taybeh, a predominantly Christian town, has worked as a teacher and in the transportation industry. She has an associate's degree and no children. She believes the thought processes in Palestinian society recently have changed and allowed women more room and freedom to get educated because society realized a woman could raise her children better, keep her house in order more efficiently, and help her husband with household and non-household decisions. "In the past," Sarah says, "a woman could not even help her child with homework and didn't know how to handle problems due to her limited education and life experiences." She also believes it is important for "the woman to have her own identity as long as it does not affect the relationship between her and her husband. A woman is part of society—a collective people whose values are based on the family."

Sarah says the greatest challenge facing Palestinian women her age is finding work. "Employers seek young women, which is a dangerous precedent to set. What about us who have more experience? We have to compete with men and young women. But there is a lack of work that not only a person my age faces but all age groups. Israel isn't allowing permits for Palestinians to open businesses or allowing Palestinians to cross into Israel for work."

Story #4—Rising above Expectations

Aisha is a thirty-year-old mother of four. She was still a student at Birzeit University when she became pregnant the first time. The remarkable part of her story is that she finished her schooling in between giving birth to three children. Her parents and in-laws took care of the kids while she studied. She would love for society to change their views that "all a woman is good for is getting married and having kids." She continues to say, "We have women in higher-powered [positions] and [they] have shown that they are capable of doing more than raising kids in life. Their opinions and advice are valuable for raising the status of the society as a whole." Aisha is pregnant with her fifth child and would like to go back to teaching when all of her children are in school.

Stories: Palestinian Monologues

Story #5—Justice for One, Justice for All

Seventy-nine-year-old Rania has been very influential in Palestinian society. She became very involved with the women's social movement in the late 1960s. She was a member of the General Union of Palestinian Women (GUPW), active in the Young Women's Christian Association (YWCA), and a member of Birzeit University's board of trustees. She also founded the National Conservatory of Music. In the early 1970s, the GUPW established a two-tiered strategy to empower women. Its agenda was to mainly confront the Israeli occupation and also provide vocational training and education to women on all subject matters. After 1993 the GUPW became more socially involved by emphasizing specific issues such as the constitution and women's laws. The organization then shifted its focus to address the occupation by supporting women who had lost their husbands to war, or whose sons and husbands were in jail. "Hand in hand, we encouraged women to become educated. We gave out scholarships. It was the political way into changing social issues. Simply telling women, 'Let's talk about women's rights' was not going to mobilize women, but the occupation is what brought them together. That's when women realized their potential, and a 'we can do more' attitude emerged."

In regard to religion, she states, "I am a Christian, and my grandfather was a Christian pastor. We went to church, but we didn't believe in all the appearances of church. We didn't embellish with crosses,

123

et cetera, at that time. We had Muslims come with us to church. All I remember is that we were Arab. Muslims and Christians were one; it was an Arab and Palestinian awakening. As Palestine became more threatened, the religious element became much more strong."

Regarding roles in society, Rania believes women "should be the conscience of any society. Women have always been much more willing to sacrifice—much more willing to have peace in the family. When you teach a child justice, the child will grow up to be just. Women know this by experience, not birth. They are the moderators and have to keep the balance in the family." She adds that she wonders why women have not been able to expand this role on a larger scale in society.

Story #6—Changing Women's Self-Perceptions: Already Good Enough!

I met a woman named Manal who is the director of a private school system in Ramallah in the West Bank. She also has worked for the UN as well as international development and relief organizations. She believes Palestinian women have stepped up to the plate and contributed to society. She says:

> They [women] proved themselves by resisting the occupation. Their leadership is very much recognized in that respect, but we've always feared that after they've taken these significant roles in politics or resisting occupation

that they go back home and go back to the kitchen. That recognition of leadership is not taken back to their homes. Now what we've seen around us is maybe due to the economic situation, where we've had to have an economic need for women to go back to work. And for that they became empowered, went back home, and demanded more respect and equality.

From that I have seen a lot of women have joined the labor market. I'm not sure they did it for the reasons they believed they should, or [that] their husbands or fathers believed in equality and wanted them out there. They were pushed into it because of the economy. With that said there are many benefits socially, because she is out there, and she becomes empowered. So [the woman] goes back home and demands respect, asking for change and equality and says, 'I'm working really hard too.'

But how much success are they getting? I'm not the one who can analyze this, nor am I an expert in this field. I've never read a study on it. But in middle-class circles, I see how my friends are dealing with it. I see how women and men's roles are shifting, and the man is taking more responsibility—pitching in with house-work and childcare—a lot more than before. So, yes, there certainly has been change.

We've also had some successful women in government, education, health, business, and politics (the mayor of Ramallah is a woman). There are lots of examples of women in higher power, although at times they are there as tokens. Men are proud to announce they have one or two token women. But these women have really proved themselves and are performing well. We hope that trend continues and women start looking beyond their roles as mothers and contribute productively to state-building [and] to civil society in general.

She goes on to say that the greatest challenges facing Palestinian women are inequality and the continued perception by society and themselves that their main role is to be child bearers and wives. She says:

I think their perception of themselves is not where it should be. They need to believe more in their potential as human beings, as change agents who are able to give back to their society in productive ways. Women don't believe they're raised with the notion 'You are a woman, and you will get a great education, great career, and do wonderful things with your life.' Very few women have that viewpoint. They are an obstacle in their own development.

Story #7—Family Sacrifice

In one Beit Liqya household we find Fatimeh, a thirty-seven-year-old who completed fourth-grade education. She got married when she was sixteen years old. Her husband remarried five years into their marriage. She implied that she was beaten until she sold her gold from their wedding (part of her dowry) so he could remarry. If she leaves, she loses rights and access to her seven children. She is unwilling to do that. "I would rather be miserable at home than leave the kids," she says.

Story #8—The Soldier Way of Life Is No Longer Lived Inside the House; There Are Only Soldiers Outside

I found life to be completely different in Ramallah, a city that is just twenty minutes away from Beit Liqya. Twenty-seven-year-old Shadia has a master's degree, works for a media company, and lives with her husband and two children. She does not believe the role of a Palestinian woman is any different than that of a Palestinian man. Shadia says:

In life and life's demands, we find that a woman can live with or without a man. She can do all the things that a man does and more, working and taking care of the household. But life without a man is much harder in our society. Today's woman has two roles—she brings in money like a man, makes decisions like a man. The "soldier" way of life is no longer lived inside the house. There are only soldiers outside.

Change is hard in Palestinian society. People here see it as, "You're going to ruin our daughters." But how is a woman going to raise her kids if her husband passes away or if he turns out to be a bad guy? If she is having major relationship issues, her parents force her to stay with him, or she is forced to send the kids to her in-laws' house while she lives in her parents' house. If she is not educated, how is she going to bring in money? There are no jobs for uneducated people; if so they go to the males first. So the person who is spending money on this disgruntled wife is the one who will tell her what to do and make decisions based on what they think is right and good, not what she wants to do. And since society does not accept her living by herself, all her hopes and dreams are put in one basket—a guy. If a woman brings in more money, she has more decision-making power.

Story #9—Power to the People

Maysa is the director of a research center in Ramallah and recently resigned as a professor at Birzeit University. She believes the regression to conservatism in Palestine in recent years stems from the events of 9/11 in New York and the second *Intifadah* in 2000. Whereas the first *Intifadah* of 1987 increased women's status in society, the events in the early 2000s gave rise to the Islamic fundamentalist movement. She says:

Nongovernmental organizations (NGOs) cropped up, which detached from the grassroots social movement. We found ourselves addressing issues that the donors wanted, not addressing the real social issues. The Palestinian leadership turned out to be more elite and detached from the masses. The elite had most of the privileges. They did not really identify with the poor women. When you talk about democracy, you need to address what the people want.

How do you answer the female who says to you, "My husband is in prison," or "My sons are in prison," or "My husband is out of work"? At that time no one cared about the elections because people's needs were not being met. There was nothing being done for the people. The seculars have not been able to solve women's problems—and there is something more that fundamentalists have been able to provide women that the secularists have not. We have a patriarchy society, especially when it comes to resources.

Women do not have access to resources like men; they aren't able to challenge the social traditions, and that's why traditions keep minimizing the role in one way or another. Women aren't able to express themselves or represent themselves.

Chapter Ten

Research Gaps and Themes

One gap not addressed in this research is the role of religion in emerging countries that could affect a society's view on work. In most Muslim families, what women are or are not allowed to do is based on traditional and cultural understandings rather than on the rights given in Islam. Even the most traditional interpretations of the Quran (the holy book of Muslims) are not in accordance with how many families treat female members, in particular when women are denied the right to inherit property or are prevented from continuing their education. Specific verses in the Quran clearly establish equality between women and men before God. Ali (1994) translates in verse 4:1:

> O men, fear your Lord who created you from a single cell, and from it created its mate, and from the two of them dispersed men and

women in multitudes. So fear God in whose name you ask of one another (the bond of) relationships. (p.73)[55]

Ali (1994) also translates a second example in verse 4:32, which states:

Do not covet what God has favoured some with more than He has some others. Men have a share in what they earn, and women have theirs in what they earn. Ask God for His favours. Surely God has knowledge of every thing. (p. 78)

A third example translated by Ali (1994) appears in verse 4:33, which proclaims:

For each We have appointed heirs to what parents and relatives leave behind. And to those you have given your pledge in marriage give their share, for God is witness to every thing. (p. 78)

There are also strong sayings by the Prophet Muhammad, or *Ahadith*, which tell parents to treat their sons and daughters justly and to educate them both. Thus it is not necessarily religion but traditional and cultural practices that diminish women, and a strong distinction must be made between what are truly religious ideologies or simply traditional practices. For example women are sometimes criticized for leaving the home and family for work, yet there is no basis in Islam for this criticism, only in traditional practice.

There is also a large Palestinian Christian population that may have different views from Palestinian Muslims. I interviewed both Christians and Muslims, but only seven out of the fifty-five women were born Christian; three are atheist, and two are agnostic. The focus of the study is on Palestinian women, regardless of religious affiliation. Future research should consider more Palestinian Christians as well as non-religious Palestinians.

Another gap is in regard to distinguishing Palestinians who live in refugee camps, Gaza, the West Bank, and in rural and urban areas. There is not enough information to see how life experiences in these regions affect society's openness to gender equality in the workplace.

A third gap that has not been addressed is how Palestinian women's lives in the workplace might change if Palestinians were completely independent from Israel. Currently Palestinians cannot build commercial or residential homes to conduct business without obtaining a business permit from Israeli authorities. Also, Palestinians who want to work in Israel must apply for permission and pay a daily fee for working with Israeli companies. This tight-fist control could be loosened if peace prevailed in the region, but it is unclear whether Palestinian women would have greater opportunity to work, as the Palestinian economy is closely tied to Israel. The economy could be suppressed even further, as witnessed in Eastern Europe when the Berlin Wall fell in 1989.

Finally the current research on the percentage of Palestinian men and women in the workplace reflects organized sectors of industries. Most of the businesses in the Palestinian territories are—and always have been—small family-owned businesses or entrepreneurial in nature. It is common and normal for Palestinian women to work in family businesses without receiving pay. Further research is needed to assess the true value of a Palestinian woman's performance in society, but this study shows that Palestinian women perceive themselves as having high social capital.

Sixteen distinct themes emerged as a result of the interviews. For the purposes of this study, I will discuss the topics where change has taken place in Palestinian society.

Gender Parity

There were several themes tied to gender parity in the women's answers, including twenty-three references to roles, eighteen to marriage, and seventeen to social capital. Palestinian men and women have different roles in society, and men are still viewed as the breadwinners. The traditional patriarchal system is still in place, which limits a woman's ability to have an equal voice in her marriage. This is especially true if she has no education or does not bring in any income. Palestinian society still focuses on the preservation of a woman's honor and reputation. Society tends to be more forgiving when men make mistakes but often punishes women for not being perfect. However, this is changing to an extent. Women are finding their voices and standing up for themselves. Most young women are delaying marriage until they graduate from college.

Younger women in Palestinian society are realizing that obtaining an education is the key to securing a better status in society, and they are putting off marriage to do so. They believe they are equal to men, even if a percentage of society has yet to fully realize that. Most older Palestinian women recognize the importance of education, although it may be too late for them to return to school. There are exceptions to this attitude, such as the divorced mother of four who went to college at the same time as her oldest son. More and more women are recognizing the importance of knowledge, and while the economy may not secure them a job, access to information allows them to raise smarter, more socially productive children.

Reproductive Capital

Society perceives women as child bearers and expects women to prioritize family over their careers. Most of women I interviewed, including all of the educated women, see themselves as playing a much larger role than giving birth and playing house. The women made thirty-one references to reproductive capital, and many of the references were linked to marriage (six), gender parity (four), roles (three), social capital (three), and social empowerment (three).

Social Empowerment

Most Palestinian women view themselves as assets to society, even if they are not earning money. My interviewees made twenty references that link social empowerment to education and educational empowerment, which suggests that higher education gives women the opportunity to do more in society. There were sixteen references to gender parity in the context that men do not value women because they are not earning money. This is a catch-22 in Palestinian society; historically a man's role in society and responsibility in marriage is to earn money and to be financially responsible for the household. However, a woman who does everything that is expected of her historically has been seen as being less than equal to her male counterpart. This suggests that while a Palestinian woman can be perfect, she will never be good enough or have an equal voice in society unless she is earning money.

Educational Empowerment

Overall, education is considered a prerequisite to better a Palestinian's life, increase nation-building, and promote future peace. In general Palestinian men and women are encouraged to go to college. The focus of a Palestinian woman is not simply to protect her family's name through honor, to obey her father, and to please her husband. Education is the key component that is needed to break down outdated traditions and provide protection from bad marriages and the Israeli occupation.

The past decade has seen a major rise in the number of women entering universities and vocational schools. More women than men are enrolled in higher education, which shows that women are linking their protection to a college degree rather than to a man. Thirteen references linked education to social empowerment, a major shift from the historical view that a woman's place is with whomever her father decides.

As one interviewee described, the soldier way of life no longer exists inside the home, only outside the home. Fewer women are obligated to take orders from their male family members, mainly because women not only provide for themselves, but also have proven they can financially contribute to help male family members. And women who are able to provide an income have greater freedom to exercise their voices and make decisions in the household.

Self Versus Collective

In my interviews the women were very specific in asking for society's help in viewing them as valuable individuals who greatly contribute to society. Palestinian women are harshly judged and punished for their mistakes, whereas men are given a slap on the wrist. Feminists have pointed out that dualistic traditions are not gender neutral; in these traditions, men, the masculine, and the rational are identified with the transcendent and immortal realm of God, while women, the feminine, and the emotional are identified with the imperfect body and the changing world that is rejected. When maleness is identified with the transcendent and spiritual, "it follows that men are more in the image of God than women and that divine power must be imaged as male rather than female. Spiritual feminists assume that women are fully equal to men and seek a spiritual vision in which women and the female body are celebrated as being in the image of God...but dualism [in societies like the Palestinians] is one of the major sources of sexism in religious thinking."[56] This way of thinking has been passed on from generation to generation, and Palestinian women must question whose religious rules they are following—the Quran or man's interpretation of the Holy Book.

Many Palestinian women also believe that in order to change society, they must change themselves. Palestinian women are not able to be part of a family unit without being tied down by it; why is permission needed from a brother, husband, or father if a woman is old enough to make her own decisions? Also, Palestinian women recently have recognized the importance of raising their sons and daughters as being equal to one another. In the interviews, women linked the issue of self versus collective to gender parity ten times, identity six times, marriage nine times, and roles seven times. Society's rules are adversely linked to social capital seven times and social empowerment nine times.

Reality Versus Perception

An overwhelming majority of the women I interviewed believe they are capable of doing anything they want, with or without a man, but are held by society's perception that they are better off with a man. Palestinian women in villages feel more restricted in their movement and worry more about preserving their honor and reputations. Again, times are changing. Today's nineteen-year-old Palestinian woman cannot relate to her mother and grandmother, whose lives revolved around manual labor. Also, times are changing as to how Palestinian youths are fighting for their freedom from the Israeli occupation. On March 7, 2012, the *Jerusalem Post*'s website published an article titled "Palestinian Non-Violent Resistance Catching On." It was a report about Sami Awad, a trainer who was "wrapping up a day of training with Palestinian women leaders in Bethlehem, another step in the effort not only to empower women, but to extend the concept and practice of non-violent popular resistance." Awad works for the Holy Land Trust in Bethlehem, "one of the most visible organizations promoting non-violent resistance as a Palestinian weapon."[57]

Fashion

Palestinian women have not always dressed in the same way in the past seventy years, but just about every Palestinian woman has a traditional dress, or *thoub*, in her closet. These days what a woman wears depends on the village or city where she grew up, how much money her parents made, and her family's beliefs regarding religion.

There was a wide range of answers when it came to the question regarding how women dressed—specifically regarding the *hijab, mandeela,* and *jilbab.* Although they were not directly asked, some women told me they wear their *hijab* voluntarily, while others said their parents enforce it. Other women wear the head covering as a fashion statement and accept the image of women in a *hijab* walking down a catwalk and attracting attention to their colorful *jilbab,* four-inch heels, and perfectly made-up eyes that are lined with black eyeliner, mascara, and teal eye shadow.

I encountered religious women who do not cover their hair and do not believe the head covering is fundamental to believing in God. Many women openly embrace the *hijab* in public and wear more liberal clothes inside their homes. In public many women feel safer wearing the *hijab* or dressing conservatively, but this movement alienates Christians, Muslims, and others who do not want to wear the *hijab.* Some Palestinian women decide to wear the *hijab* later in life, due to their becoming more religious or wanting to fit in with their age group and society's norm of older women covering up.

Fashion statements come and go; Western and European-style outfits are highly prevalent in Palestinian culture, but the movement toward conservative attire in the last ten years has polarized the region. There is no law that forces women to dress a certain way, but in a patriarchal society, we find that social norms supersede the laws of the court system. I had the opportunity to attend two weddings from upper-class families and observed a mixture of styles that ranged from short skirts and shoulder-bearing outfits to black attire from head to toe.

Religion

Most Palestinians are born with the notion that religion is the compass that guides them through life. Asking whether religion is important to a Palestinian is like asking if two eyes are better than one. "It's how we're born," one interviewee says. Not all Palestinians agree. Nine interviewees do not believe a person needs to be religious to have faith. There are also Palestinians who believe religion is the source of conflict and bloodshed, not enlightenment.

It was difficult to decipher which women are enlightened from within to follow God and which are following a man's version of how a woman should act and dress to be a good Muslim or Christian. It also is unclear whether the conservative movement will continue in the Palestinian territories and how that will affect women's religious values.

Role Models

When it comes to female role models, the women I interviewed don't feel they have anyone to look up to, but they also have a different perception of what constitutes a role model. Unlike in the United States, where actresses, actors, celebrities, leaders, journalists, and successful businesspeople are considered role models, Palestinian women do not seek fame, glory, or attention for their accomplishments. For the most part, they look at other women who are bettering themselves and their communities. This seemed like an unusual question for the women to answer, perhaps because Muslims are not supposed to idolize individuals.

However, both Muslims and Christians declined to answer this question. The lack of responses could be viewed as a "lack of voice" issue, or it could be a way to imply resentment for colonialization by the West.

Forty-six out of fifty-five women said they did not have any role models while growing up. Not surprisingly the few interviewees who gave commentary regarding role models linked the issue to social capital (two) and social empowerment (two).

Palestinian and American Similarities and Differences

Do many Palestinian women believe there are similarities and differences between Palestinian and American women? The answer is yes to both. Most of the differences women cited were positive. Palestinian women view American women as self-empowered individuals who are able to change their circumstances and do not require permission from men. However, Palestinian women also believe American women are still struggling for equality, like women in many other cultures.

Many Palestinian women believe that women are women, regardless of where they come from, and are looking to raise healthy families, have successful careers, and be in secure relationships. Although my interviewees did not specify which type of American women they were referring to, people in Palestinian society refer to Americans as "white" by default and specify other ethnicities (African-American, Arab-American, Latino, etcetera.) when necessary.

Also it is unclear why so many women did not respond to this question, except that many women had not personally interacted with American women and could not think of how they were similar or different. It could be that Palestinian women can only identify with American women in the context of conflict, and perhaps they do not feel supported in the Palestinian-Israeli conflict or do not feel a bond of sisterhood with American women. They also might feel a resistance to Western colonialization at a deep social-psychological level. More open-ended follow-up questions, such as, "Are there similarities or differences between Palestinian women and women in other countries? If so, which countries and why?" may have provided more insight into the lack of responses to the question.

A number of factors have contributed to the shift in Palestinian women's perceptions of themselves and their roles in society, including the rise in education for males and females, Internet usage, and social media connections with the rest of the world. Along with this is the basic need, more than ever, to feel appreciated and to participate fully in society—within Palestinian communities and the outside world.

The Israeli occupation has limited Palestinian and Israeli growth potential, and a comprehensive discussion of the Israeli occupation and its psychological, socioeconomic, and political effects on Palestinians and Israelis would require writing another book. Yet the situation of Palestinian women cannot be fully understood without comprehending the dimensions of the historical disasters that have befallen them since the beginning of the twentieth century, and especially since 1948. The occupation is one landmark within a series of catastrophic landmarks that loom threateningly over every single aspect of Palestinian lives. Women are at the forefront in facing those events and suffering their consequences.

Conclusion

Blessing in Movement

We have looked at how Palestinian women have evolved during the last seventy years in Palestinian society, their roles in the domestic sphere and the labor market, society's perception of Palestinian women, and women's perceptions of themselves. We have discussed the importance of religion, marriage, identity, work, and self-autonomy in these women's lives.

Palestinian society and the status of Palestinian women are in a transient stage that is subject to many influences. Foremost among these is the political situation and the continuous process of dispossession and denial of identity to which they are being subjected, which exacerbates the impact of other factors, such as tradition and faith. It is also interesting to note, however, that this situation has given impetus to many women casting away the fetters of tradition, while others find in religion and dress (the *hijab* and *thoub*) a means to confront their threatened identities.

We also have examined how the *hijab* is used both as a fashion statement and a religious symbol. We have read firsthand stories of Palestinian women's lives and the intricately linked themes that are woven into the Palestinian lifestyle. Sixteen themes emerged; we find that no one theme stands alone. Education, for example, is the key to unlocking many doors, not just one. Learning to read and write has socioeconomic, political, and socio-psychological effects that may not be fully measured through a formal exam but by future life experiences.

Although Palestinian women have made great achievements in education, this has not translated into full freedoms and the ability to making personal decisions without judgment or shame from their families or communities. Many people in the world live their lives in doubt, fear, shame, guilt, or a combination of these feelings, and Palestinian women are no different. However, Palestinian women have the added burden of fighting traditions that take them on a path they may not have chosen for themselves. The ongoing conflict since 1948 also has overshadowed the need to properly address social issues that affect both Palestinian men and women.

Palestinian women are still fighting to be heard and to prove their worth in society. Many Palestinian women are undervalued and underpaid, and they lack the social freedoms that men enjoy. Society could see far greater benefits by using all of its human capital. The good news is that Palestinian women are determined to make themselves heard and to carve their places in society, no matter how long it takes. They know that Palestinian women are traditionally perceived to be the custodians of their society's boundaries. In other words they take care of the day-to-day household chores, cook, clean, and give birth to children, but they do not make financial decisions and are discouraged from voicing their opinions about making decisions for themselves. Based on mainstream coverage that fails to account for Palestinians' own perspectives, many people assume Palestinians are generally illiterate and live to fight, not fight to live. The Western perception is that there is a one-size-fits all cookie-cutter image of a Palestinian man and woman. This perception often is a byproduct of listening to media coverage rather than listening to Palestinians themselves. Second, there is a lack of literature that reflects Palestinian women's belief systems, opinions, and thoughts. Palestinian women historically have been perceived as child bearers, not as mothers or wives. They do not receive credit for their achievements, nor do they seek to be in the spotlight. Third, most studies conducted in research centers and universities in the West Bank are in Arabic, which may not be accessible by Internet or translated into English or other commonly spoken languages. Fourth, tourists who visit Jerusalem and the surrounding areas usually do not cross over into Palestinian territories, which limits their perceptions regarding what they see on the Israeli side, an area that enjoys the lifestyle of a first-world country.

Things are changing, however. There is a growing intolerance for corrupt, broken regimes and patriarchal dominance in the Middle East. Templates that have governed Arab countries and dictated women's behavior in society are changing. The voices of Arab women are no longer kept in jars and are being heard loud and clear in Tahrir Square, alongside men who come from all parts of society. They range from the poorest farmer to a young Google executive, all of whom share the same need for freedom and dignity. In fact the term "Dignity Revolution," or *Thawrat al Karam* in Arabic, is a more accurate description of how the Middle East views the recent social revolts against their governments. In February 2012 *The Huffington Post* published an article by Maytha Alhassen titled "Please Reconsider the Term 'Arab Spring,' " which states, "These movements are more than just a 'democratic blooming'—they are what democracy is predicated on, a revolutionary demand for recognizing their right to human dignity."[58]

Egyptian women were once told to go home and raise presidents but not to run for president. This thinking only encouraged more women to join the nonviolent Egyptian revolution. But what changes can Palestinians, especially women, bring to their situation? Palestinian women, too, have been active in promoting the welfare of their people and fighting for their land (as early as 1917 but most notably since the 1964 formation of the Palestinian

Liberation Organization). However, dramatic shifts in perception of gender issues among women did not change until the 1970s. Today politicians and men in Palestine no longer can stamp their names on wheat fields, olive groves, and agreements that serve their personal agendas. Four generations of Palestinians have inherited tents of exile, displaced emotions, and a reputation of being terrorists who treat their women poorly.

If this study had been conducted seventy years ago, what are the chances that an eighteen- or eighty-year-old woman would have been open to—or capable of—sharing her desires and needs besides the importance of finding a husband, raising children, and working in the fields? There is no doubt that Palestinian women live in a time and place where family is fundamental to life. The need for family stems from traditional and cultural origins, or *hamula*, as well as social and national solidarity. This is still the case in many Palestinian villages, but more and more Palestinian women are recognizing how much they contribute to society without needing to follow outdated traditions in the domestic or economic sphere.

Closing the gender gap in the workplace will not happen overnight, but women in emerging markets are making room for themselves in the global market. This is not about women overpowering men, but about finding greater equality, freedom, and value for the work they provide to a relationship inside and outside the home. Also, with limited jobs in the Palestinian market and high unemployment rates, it is difficult to match jobs with the increased number of female graduates. Women are encouraged to branch out from work roles in healthcare, agriculture, and lower-management positions. More and more Palestinian women are working in unconventional fields and doing jobs that were once typically reserved for men, such as becoming racecar drivers. In 2010 National Public Radio presented a story titled "In the West Bank, Women With a Need for Speed," which described a group of female Palestinian racecar drivers called the Speed Sisters. Mona Enab, a twenty-four-year-old former beauty pageant contestant, is one of those drivers. This sport is growing in popularity with Palestinian women.

Another field that is emerging is the rap music scene. Who would have thought there would be a female Palestinian rapper? Her name is Abeer Alzanaty (aka Sabreena da Witch), and while there have been reports that point to a dozen new rap groups in the conservative region of Gaza, Abeer emerged as the first female rapper. She also is featured in the documentary *Slingshot Hip Hop*. Whereas displaced Palestinians inside Israel are facing discrimination, Abeer gained support after being fired from a well-known fast food chain for speaking Arabic. In the film she is encouraged to talk about it—or rather, rap about it—in a song called *"Sawt al-Samt"* ("The Sound of Silence"). According to *The Electronic Intifada*, the film relates that despite support from her parents, Abeer was dissuaded from performing with Tamer and Suhell (her cousins, who also are featured in the documentary) on television by strong opposition from some of her extended family. Despite her disappointment, she continues to practice her lyrics at home. "I'm just doing it because there's no other reason to live," Abeer explains, and eventually joins her cousins on stage.[59]

Abeer's story shows how strong an extended family's influence can be on a Palestinian woman's life and her need to fight for what she wants in her life. In 2009 Abeer took her ten-year collection of songs and produced a fifteen-track album. In 2010 *Electronic Intifada* published an online article titled "Sabreena da Witch: The First Lady of Palestinian R&B." The article states:

> "All of the songs are written from the point of view of a woman who's a witch, who happens to be a woman of color, who happens to be a Palestinian," she explained. But it's not only Alzinaty's identity that motivates her to rap about such issues in her music. "I don't believe in boxes; if Palestine was not under occupation, I probably wouldn't be talking about it. It has nothing to do with me being Palestinian, but more with me feeling that this is wrong—the way Israel is [behaving] is just not OK."[60]

Women such as Nisreen Awwad also are making an impact in Palestinian society. Originally from the Qalandiya refugee camp, Awwad produces the first women's radio show dedicated solely to women's issues. The show is called *Nisaa FM* ("*nisaa*" means women in Arabic) and is almost entirely run by women.

Artistic expression is another area in which Palestinian women shine. Palestinians always have applied the arts in their daily lives. Despite the current political turmoil, we find dozens of visual art, theater, film, and dance organizations in Palestine representing Palestinian artists. Visual art organizations such as Al-Ma'mal, Al Hosh in Jerusalem, A.M. Qattan Foundation, Khalil Sakakini Cultural Center, Goethe Institute, and Al Mahatta in Ramallah serve to nurture and support artists of all backgrounds in Palestine. [61, 62, 63, 64, 65, 66]

Shashat, which means "screens" in Arabic, is a nongovernmental organization that focuses on women's cinema. Shashat recently hosted a women's film festival that featured more than one hundred screenings in cities throughout the West Bank and Gaza. The festival showed ten films by women—and about women—in order to highlight the role of female talent in the occupied territories. [67]

Eltiqa Group for Contemporary Art in Gaza encourages Palestinians to express themselves through the paintbrush. [68] Artist Amal Adelrahman, born in Jabalia refugee camp in Gaza, has participated in many local exhibitions. [69] In addition Tina Sherwell completed her PhD on Palestinian art and has written articles on Palestinian art and culture. She is based in Jerusalem, where she has worked with local art centers and galleries and currently works as a freelance curator and writer.

The truth may be that the pen is mightier than the sword, especially for Sahar Khalifeh, who is considered to be one of the most prominent Palestinian authors in the last eighty years. One of her best-known works is the novel *Wild Thorns,* and she won the 2006 Naguib Mahfouz Medal for Literature for her novel *The Image, the Icon, and the Convenant.* Liana Badr's short story "Other Cities" takes readers on a hazardous journey by service taxis from old Hebron to Ramallah that is littered with military checkpoints. Huzama Habayeb's story "A Thread Snaps" earned notoriety for its direct way in handling the subject of a girl's growing awareness of her bodily desires.

When it comes to cinema, Al-Kasaba Theater in Ramallah is the only formal film venue for the nearly 2.5 million Palestinians living in the West Bank.[70] Gaza doesn't have a theater. Barely any formal funding is available, but we do find female Palestinian directors such as Annemarie Jacir (*Salt of This Sea*) and Etimad Wshah, a Gazan and the first female director to train men and women on how to carry cameras in the streets of Gaza.[71]

We also find fascinating women such as Rima Nassir Tarazi, who has incorporated art into her life and promoted it throughout society. Music was her passion early in life, and she began to compose at age eleven. Rima was born in 1932 in Jaffa, Palestine, to parents from Birzeit, whose family would establish a school that later would be developed into what is now Birzeit University. She started her music education at age seven with renowned Palestinian musicians Salvador Arnita and Hanna Khatchadourian (known later as Ohan Durian Nnarc). Arnita and Ohan gave Rima piano lessons and conducted the school choir. In 1947 she pursued her education at the American Junior College in Beirut, where she studied harmony and took private piano lessons.

After obtaining her sophomore degree in 1949, Rima went to Paris to pursue musical studies. She took piano lessons with two formidable teachers, Marie Le Duc and Lucette Descaves, and composition at École César-Franck. She had to interrupt her studies early in 1951 to return to Birzeit, where her aunt, Nabiha Nasir, founder of Birzeit University, was dying. She stayed there until 1952 to help teach music and compose songs for the college choir, in addition to taking on cultural activities in general and teaching other subjects. In 1952 she received a bachelor's degree from the American University of Beirut in psychology and Arabic. From 1954 to 1956, she taught music at Birzeit University and composed songs alongside the renowned musician Yusef Batroni and the young composer Amin Nasser.

In 1956 Rima married Antone Tarazi. They moved to Canada, where he conducted neurosurgical training in Montreal. In 1960 the family settled in Palestine, where her husband established a neurosurgical center in Jerusalem.

After 1967 Rima became heavily involved in community work and activism in a number of women's societies and cultural and educational organizations.

Through her music and songs, she strived to invest hope and resilience in her people, who lived under Israeli occupation, and to tell the story of her people to the world. She continued to compose for renowned poets, but later she embarked upon writing her own lyrics for children and adults, which were inspired by her personal experiences and the firsthand testimonies of her people's struggle for freedom and justice. She and her sister-in-law, soprano Tania Tamari Nasir, performed these songs in several Palestinian venues and abroad, which would be produced as *The Dreams of My People* in 1986 and later recorded as a CD titled *Ila Mata (Until When)* in 2006.

In 1993 Rima—with colleagues Salwa Tabri, Amin Nasser, Nadia Aboushi, and Suhail Khoury—founded the National Conservatory of Music, under the umbrella of Birzeit University, a landmark event in Rima's life and in the cultural life of Palestine. In 2004, as a tribute to the invaluable cultural and intellectual contributions to humanity of the late Edward Said, the name of the conservatory was changed to the Edward Said National Conservatory of Music.

Despite Palestinians' love for art, the paradox between religion and fashion is what usually makes headlines. Is the conservatism a mask, a way to wear the symbol but still fight against the oppressive ideology? In Middle Eastern societies, it can be difficult to tell who is really religious and spiritual and who is not. In April 2010 *Foreign Policy* published an article in which it defines and describes religion in the following manner.

Etymologists tell us that the word "religion" may come from the Latin root *religare*, meaning to adhere or bind. It's a wonderful derivation. In both its secular and religious manifestations, faith is alluring and seductive precisely because it's driven by propositions that bind or adhere the believer to a compelling set of ideas that satisfy rationally or spiritually, but always obligate.[72]

When it comes to the *hijab*, however, we find another purpose besides adherence to religion. In Egypt, for example, the expression of sexuality remains a taboo. Mona Abaza, a sociology professor at the American University in Cairo, believes that by adapting sexy outfits to the *hijab*, young women are attempting to be veiled and appealing at the same time. "Many women have picked up on the hijab-chic trend and started grooming businesses where veiled women can have their scarves arranged for different occasions - from graduation parties to weddings," writes Dina Abdel-Maged in the Al Jazeera article, *The Multiple Shades of the Hijab.*[73]

She also reports that "thanks to long-sleeved, close-fitting tops, veiled women can buy any piece of clothing, from strapless tops to backless dresses." Noha Maarouf, a social psychologist in Cairo, believes that the "*hijab* has turned into a social phenomenon that does not necessarily reflect religiosity." Maarouf goes on to say, "Many people are rallying behind the superficial aspects of religion because of the absence of a common cause.... In the past, less women wore *hijab*, but people were definitely more religious than today. Ethics are the core of religion, not appearance."[74]

The perception of women—by women and men—also must change. It is impossible to control the political landscape in countries, but women are focusing on what they can control. Women all over the world, regardless of how progressive they have become, are still seeking change. The story of emerging markets is one of rags to riches, or releasing the mute button on women when they are in the room. It is a time when the daughter is rising, with or without the permission of the family. Women in Palestinian society emerged not because men told them it was OK to do so, but because life placed demands on them to step up and show their power. Palestinian men, the main breadwinners of families, became imprisoned or died due to the Israeli occupation. Women, who had little education, had to find a way to feed their families; they had to take on what traditionally had been considered a man's role. However, there was no need for women to fight too hard; the economic hardships they endured on a daily basis motivated them to earn an income and fight for the security of their families.

Seventy years ago most Palestinian women did not go to school for several reasons. First, Palestinians were mainly an agricultural society, where very little money was made. Schools in the villages went up to the fourth grade, and later to the eighth grade; any additional education had to be completed in larger cities such as Ramallah and Jerusalem. Parents barely made enough money to put food on the table, let alone pay for books, uniforms, and a bus ride so their daughters could go to school. Only daughters of bourgeois families were encouraged to go to school and work. Also the Palestinian work environment was not set up to support women. Regardless of how much education a female eventually received, the knowledge would not be used beyond the boundaries of taking care of the house and raising children. This study, however, shows that times are changing. The soldier way of life of taking orders from soldiers and Israel is being checked at the door. Thanks to education, women are taking on more responsibility to help balance the power inside the home.

The big question regarding Palestinian women is "What is holding them back from stepping into their full power?" The answer may be simple, but it is fundamental to their cause—movement or lack thereof. The lack of movement enforced on a woman within Arab societies and the Israeli restrictions placed on Palestinians fundamentally take away a Palestinian woman's choice to do what she wants with her life. It is a system that places limitations on a person's psyche, a social system that treats males better than females, and is reinforced by mothers who give preferential treatment to their sons. Women must learn to raise their girls to be equal to boys in all ways.

In the last seventy years, Palestinian women slowly have gained respect in their communities, but they have a long way to go. The good news is that many Palestinian women recognize the importance of change, and they are starting to make sacrifices to help the lives of other Palestinian women; they are not simply trying to please men. In the past, society may have ignored them, but women cannot be ignored. They are human beings who work hard inside and outside of their homes. Women are the foundation and gatekeepers of society. A Palestinian woman is made in Palestine, so why does she deny herself a place at the dining room table? If she cooked the meal, she should not be the last one to sit down to eat. Palestinian women give so much of their lives to support and maintain the wellbeing of others. Giving back to themselves allows for greater opportunity for them to play a much larger role in society—much larger than the limitations Palestinian women place on themselves and allow society to place on them.

I believe a Palestinian woman's love runs as deep a two-million-meter well filled to the top. But what good is a well if it runs out of water? What many Palestinian women may not understand is that their value in society is worth more than gold. It's worth pure water—water that nourishes fathers, mothers, sons, daughters, husbands, and in-laws, as well as livestock and plants. Its water is what they build homes with, and use to cook, clean, and bathe. Without it there would be no life on earth. They carry the seeds of co-creation, growth, and compassion. This makes women more than half of society, because they take care of all of society.

The Palestinian woman is a fascinating combination of strength, sacrifice, and passion. Perhaps the greatest blessing a Palestinian can realize is that there is *fil harakah barikah* (blessing in movement).[75] Finding ways to move themselves forward will change not only Palestinian society's perception of itself, but also the world's perception of it. The world may become less fearful of a society if it can view it from multiple lenses. Perhaps the world may find that the Palestinians are proud people who are looking for the same freedoms, successes, and achievements that everyone else wants.

Like women around the world, Palestinian women have struggled to find their place in society. Palestinian women have endured verbal, physical, and emotional abuse. The added challenge is growing up in an occupied land, where every Palestinian dreams of freeing himself or herself from the chains of national conflict. Palestinian women take that challenge one step further, as they live in a society that does not fully value a woman's opinions, contributions, and desires. This is not how all Palestinian women are treated, but regardless of a Palestinian woman's place in society—whether she has a fifth-grade education or a master's degree—one thing is clear. Palestinian women desire more freedom as well as the ability to choose their own paths in life and to choose whether to be married or to live alone. Like Hilma Granqvist, the Finnish anthropologist who went to Palestine in the 1920s to observe a culture, I believe that stories, traits, and characteristics of living people in a community can offer perspective regarding wider human truths and deeper insights than what is portrayed regarding Arabs in general.

Which roles will the future Palestinian woman embrace? The answer, perhaps, lies within her. Based on the women's voices represented in this book, it is clear that it is up to each Palestinian woman to decide that for herself, as well as her desire to change society and work with men to change their beliefs about women so that all can reach a full state of dignity.

"We need to look at each other as better human beings instead of looking at women as the weaker ones in society. No, I don't see women having or being less than a man. We are equal in the eyes of God."

—*Um Basil, seventy-one years old and married for fifty-three years*

References

1   "Um" means "mother of" in Arabic. "Abu" means "father of" in Arabic. It is traditional to address a Palestinian or Arab parent as the mother or father of the oldest son's name.

2   This is an Arab proverb that suggests that one family member's actions are a reflection of the entire family.

3   The word "thwaab" is the plural of "thoub" and is the traditional Palestinian costume or dress.

4   http://weekly.ahram.org.eg/2001/535/cu1.htm

5   http://weekly.ahram.org.eg/2001/535/cu1.htm

6   Lutfiyya, A. 1956. *Baytin, a Jordanian Village: A Study of Social Institutions and Social Change in a Folk Community*. United Kingdom: The Hague, 32–34.

7   This is an Arab proverb that encourages women to be married rather than remain single.

8   The *Intifadah* (1988–1993) was the first Palestinian uprising against the Israeli occupation. The Palestinians employed nonviolent civil-disobedience methods to resist the occupation, including boycotts on Israeli products, demonstrations, self-expression in the form of art and graffiti, and refusal to pay taxes. Many people incorrectly define the *Intifadah* as the acts of youths who threw stones during this period.

9   "*Intifadat*" is the plural of "*Intifadah*," which, translated to English, means "uprising." It refers to the Palestinian uprising against the Israeli occupation. However, the word "*intifadah*" literally means "shaken" in Arabic.

10   CIA World Factbook, retrieved on November 3, 2012 from https://www.cia.gov/library/publications/the-world/geos/we.html and https://www.cia.gov/library/publications/the-world/geos/gz.html

11   Lutfiyya. "Baytin, a Jordanian Village: A Study of Social Institutions and Social Change in a Folk Community," 34.

12   http://www.passia.org

13   This is an Arab proverb that explains the importance of having a woman to deal with domestic affairs.

14   Meat usually was available during the two yearly holidays, *Eid al-Fitr* and *Eid al-Adha.*

15   See Eric Wolf's work on agrarian societies.

16   Unfortunately, due to the Israeli-Palestinian conflict, the region has not experienced peace for four generations. Since the state of Israel was created in 1948, Palestinian displacement and national politics continue to cast a shadow over the lives of people who want to live peacefully.

17   According to Israeli and Palestinian law, it is illegal for a man to be married to more than one woman, but a religious ceremony may be performed in Judaism or Islam to bless the new union. Often, though, individuals are not religious but seek the blessing of religious institutions for society to approve the new arrangement.

18   Forty-three Palestinian women in this study identified themselves as Muslim, seven as Christians, three as atheists, and two as agnostics.

19   Upbin, B. "A Young Doctor Fights the Depression Epidemic in Palestine." *Forbes*. http://www.

forbes.com/sites/bruceupbin/2013/02/27/
a-young-doctor-fights-the-depression-epidemic-
in-palestine (accessed March 20, 2013).

20   Velloso, A. 1996. "Women, Society and
Education in Palestine." *International Review
of Education* 42: 525–527.

21   Greenberg, E. 2004. "Educating Muslim
Girls in Mandatory Jerusalem." *International
Journal of Middle East Studies* 36.

22   Velloso. "Women, Society and Education in
Palestine," 525.

23   http://www.pwrdc.ps/index.php?page=
detail&p=66

24   Velloso. "Women, Society and Education in
Palestine," 526–527.

25   Davies, C. "Middle East Women Beat Men in
Education, Lose Out at Work." CNN. http://
www.cnn.com/2012/06/01/world/meast/
middle-east-women-education/index.html
(accessed June 6, 2012).

26   Shabaneh, L. and Al Saleh, J. "Palestinian
Women's Participation in the Labor Market
Challenges and Required Interventions: A
Quantitative and Qualitative Study of Women's
Participation in Labor Market." Palestinian

Women's Research and Documentation Center. http://www.pwrdc.ps/site_files/PCBS%20 STUDY.pdf (accessed November 10, 2011).

27   Shabaneh and Al Saleh, *"Palestinian Women's Participation,"* 4.

28   Women and Labor Fact Sheet. Palestinian Women's Research and Documentation Center. http://www.pwrdc.ps/?page=fact (accessed November 10, 2011).

29   Shabaneh and Al Saleh. *"Palestinian Women's Participation,"* 5.

30   Shabaneh and Al Saleh. *"Palestinian Women's Participation,"* 6.

31   Ghada Talhami, *"Occupation, War, and Feminist Perspectives: The Case of Palestinian Women,"* D. K. Pearsons Professor of Politics, Emerita. Lake Forest College, Illinois, 2011: 34-35.

32   The G7 economies comprise of Canada, Japan, Germany, France, Italy, the United Kingdom and the United States. They are the seven formerly largest wealthiest nations and meet several times a year to discuss economic policies.

33   Kanani, R. "Winning the War for Talent in Emerging Markets: Why Women Are the Solution." *Forbes.* http://www.forbes.com/

sites/rahimkanani/2011/09/06/winning-the-war-for-talent-in-emerging-markets-why-women-are-the-solution/3 (accessed September 6, 2011).

34   "The Palestinian War-Torn Economy: Aid, Development and State Formation" (presented at the United Nations Conference on Trade and Development on April 5, 2006). http://www.unctad.org/en/docs/gdsapp20061_en.pdf (accessed September 6, 2011).

35   http://parc-us-pal.org

36   Allen, D. 2010. "An Alternative Method for Assessing the Value of Housewife Services." *American Journal of Family Law* 23: 219–223.

37   Allen, "An Alternative Method," 221–222.

38   Benhold, K. "The Stigma of Being a Housewife." *The New York Times.* http://www.nytimes.com/2010/07/21/world/europe/21iht-LETTER.html?_r=1 (accessed September 6, 2011).

39   Lutfiyya. "Baytin, a Jordanian Village: A Study of Social Institutions and Social Change in a Folk Community," 32–34.

40   The Arab proverb "life offers a thousand blessings" emphasizes the existence of good people who look to help others without expectations of anything in return.

41   Lutfiyya. "Baytin, a Jordanian Village: A Study of Social Institutions and Social Change in a Folk Community," 32–34.

42   "*Nakba*" is an Arabic word that means "catastrophe" in English.

43   Houtman, G. 2007. "Interview with Akbar Ahmed." *Anthropology Today* 23: 17–19.

44   Dawkins, M. A. 2013. *Clearly Invisible: Racial Passing and the Color of Cultural Identity.* Waco, TX: Baylor University Press, xi–33.

45   "The Veil." PBS. http://www.pbs.org/wgbh/globalconnections/mideast/questions/women (accessed January 15, 2012).

46   Kawar, W. K. 1980. "The Traditional Palestinian Costume." *Journal of Palestine Studies* 10: 118–129.

47   News reports include the following sources:

      McGirk, T. May 3, 2007. Palestinian Moms Becoming Martyrs. *Time.* Retrieved on February 5, 2012 from http://www.time.com/

time/magazine/article/0,9171,1617542,00.
html

Leung, R. February 11, 2009. The Bomber
Next Door. *CBS News.* Retrieved on February
5, 2012 from http://www.cbsnews.com/2100-
3475_162-555401.html

Handwerk, B. December 13, 2004. Female
Suicide Bombers: Dying to Kill. *National
Geographic.* Retrieved on February 5, 2012
from http://news.nationalgeographic.com/
news/2004/12/1213_041213_tv_suicide_
bombers.html.

48   Abdulhadi, R. 1989. "The Palestinian
      Women's Autonomous Movement:
      Emergence, Dynamics, and Challenges."
      Gender and Society 12: 649–675.

49   Abu-Lughod, L. 1998. *Remaking Women:
      Feminism and Modernity in the Middle East.*
      Princeton, NJ: Princeton University Press,
      89–101.

50   Sayigh, R. 1986. "Encounters with Palestinian
      Women Under Occupation." *Journal of
      Palestinian Studies* 100: 3–26.

51   Sayigh, "Encounters with Palestinian
      Women," 5.

52   Velloso, "Women, Society and Education in Palestine," 529.

53   Abdulhadi, "The Palestinian Women's Autonomous Movement," 656.

54   Velloso, "Women, Society and Education in Palestine," 528.

55   Ali, A. 1994. *Al-Qur'an: A Contemporary Translation*. Princeton, NJ: Princeton University Press.

56   Christ, C. P. 2006. "Ecofeminism and Process Philosophy." *Feminist Theology* 14: 289–310.

57   O'Sullivan, A. "Palestinian Non-Violent Resistance Catching On." *Jerusalem Post*. http://www.jpost.com/Features/InThespotlight/Article.aspx?id=257932 (accessed November 10, 2012).

58   Alhassen, M. "Please Reconsider the Term 'Arab Spring.' " *The Huffington Post*. http://www.huffingtonpost.com/maytha-alhassen/please-reconsider-arab-sp_b_1268971.html (accessed March 1, 2012).

59   Murphy, M. C. "Film Review: *Slingshot Hip Hop*." The Electronic Intifada. http://electronicintifada.net/content/film-review-

slingshot-hip-hop/3541 (accessed November 10, 2011).

60   Tabar, T. "Sabreena da Witch: The First Lady of Palestinian R&B." The Electronic Intifada. http://electronicintifada.net/content/sabreena-da-witch-first-lady-palestinian-rb/8771 (accessed March 1, 2012).

61   http://www.almamalfoundation.org

62   http://www.alhoashgallery.org

63   http://www.qattanfoundation.org/en/index.asp

64   http://www.sakakini.org

65   http://www.goethe.de/enindex.htm

66   http://www.trianglenetwork.org/partners/al-mahatta

67   Odgaard, L. "A Woman Is a Sponge...Women's Film Festival in Palestine." *EMAJ Magazine.* http://emajmagazine.com/2013/01/13/a-woman-is-a-sponge-womens-film-festival-in-palestine (accessed February 1, 2013).

68   http://www.eltiqa.com

69   http://www.palestine-art.com/artists/Amaal.html

70   Woldt, M. "Palestinian Filmmakers Beat the Odds to Hit Silver Screen." CNN. http://edition.cnn.com/2009/SHOWBIZ/Movies/04/22/palestinian.territories.cinema.challenges/index.html (accessed November 10, 2011).

71   Almeghari, R. "In Gaza, Women Filmmakers Find Strength Behind the Camera." The Electronic Intifada. http://electronicintifada.net/content/gaza-women-filmmakers-find-strength-behind-camera/8267 (accessed November 1, 2011).

72   Miller, A. D. "The False Religion of Mideast Peace," *Foreign Policy,* May, 2010, http://www.foreignpolicy.com/articles/2010/04/19/the_false_religion_of_mideast_peace?page=0,6 (accessed November 1, 2011).

73   Abdel-Mageed, D. "The Multiple Shades of the Hijab." *Al Jazeera.* http://www.aljazeera.com/focus/2008/09/20089812812445443.html (accessed November 1, 2011).

74   Abdel-Mageed, D. "The Multiple Shades of the Hijab."

75   This Arab proverb states, "In movement there is blessing," meaning that one should continue to take steps forward to secure one's livelihood.

Acknowledgments

With love and gratitude, I would like to thank the following people for their support:

Ataana Badilli, Tammy Badilli, Marcia Alesan Dawkins, Ted Domville, Sejal Gala Gandhi, Moe Hamdan, Trevor Hutchins, Ramzi Jaber, Susan Jellissen, Jamie Jensen, Jeffrey Johnson, Cary Kostka, Matthew Oaks, Andrew Phay, Joleen Pursley, Robbie Pinter, Keith Sturges, and Lisa Hocking Wagner.

Special thanks to:

Kate Ransohoff, Sandy Simpson, The Cradleboard Foundation, Rima Tarazi, Belmont University, Birzeit University and the Institute of Women's Studies, The Palestinian American Research Center (PARC), and to all the Palestinian women who let me into their homes and hearts.

Finally, the following words are dedicated to anyone looking to overcome limitations and rise to his or her full potential:

May the longtime sun
Shine upon you
All love surround you
And the pure light within you
Guide your way on
Guide your way on*

* *lyrics from the Kundalini Yoga sunshine song*

Stay Connected

Book Website: www.PalestinianWomenRising.com

Facebook: www.facebook.com/palestinianwomenrising

Sharp Thinking Communications: www.Sharp
ThinkingCommunications.com

Portfolio: www.sadiquahamdan.com

Email Sadiqua: sadiqua.hamdan@gmail.com

Follow Sadiqua on Twitter: @sadiquahamdan